Accolades for
Inside the Magic Kingdom

"This is not only a fascinating behind-the-scenes look at what makes the Magic Kingdom tick, but the lessons can be applied to enhance the success of any company.**"**

Larry King
Larry King Live, CNN

"As a former editor of *Eyes and Ears*—the Walt Disney World employee newspaper—and having worked for Disney for twelve years, I am impressed by how accurately this book captures the heart of how Disney does business. More important, today as vice president of two international corporations, I found this book absolutely riveting. If you want to jump start the customer focus of *your* organization, buy a copy for yourself and every single one of your managers.**"**

Dent Thompson
Vice President
Phoenix Air Group, Inc.
Midway Phoenix Corporation

"Right on target! No matter what kind of non-profit organization you work for, if you want to take quality and value to another level, this lively and informative book is for you. It's full of insights for generating support from stakeholders.**"**

Greta A. Williams
Executive Director
Big Brothers Big Sisters of Greater Kalamazoo

"*Inside the Magic Kingdom* captures the heart and soul of one of the world's most customer-focused cultures. For a small investment of time and money, you'll reap tremendous rewards. An essential book for leaders at all levels in both profit and non-profit organizations.**"**

Pamela Dodd
President
Culture Consulting, Inc.

"If you want to find out who the most important person on a winning team is, make a copy of Lesson 7 and give it to everyone. Not only will it change the way you see the world, it will change the way the world sees you.**"**

Rocky Bleier
Former Star Running Back
Pittsburgh Steelers

"A provocative book on an enchanting subject. It's a compelling read that provides effective tools for developing your business. This will be a big book.**"**

Jack Covert
President
Schwartz Business Books

"Great book! If you want to grow your small or medium-sized company into a larger or more profitable one, buy a copy for yourself and every one of your key players right now! Use the Leader's Tool Kit to put into practice what this book preaches. The cultural evolution that follows will amaze you! **"**

Rodger Ford
Founder
AlphaGraphics Printshops of the Future

"Although the trip inside the Magic Kingdom is fascinating, the real power of this book lies in the way it forces you to look inside your own company and own behavior. It's a 'must-read' for anyone who wants to strengthen relationships with customers. **"**

Marty Carroll
Senior Vice President of Managed Care
Merck and Company

"*Inside the Magic Kingdom* is the most 'edutaining' business book in years! Tom Connellan has crafted a superb true-to-life account that entertains us with real-life stories and educates us with practical lessons from the world's most successful maker of dreams come true. Walt Disney would be extremely proud. **"**

Jim Kouzes
Co-author of *The Leadership Challenge* and *Credibility*
Chairman and CEO
Tom Peters Group/Learning Systems

"As a former Dean of Disney University, it was a treat to read *Inside the Magic Kingdom*. This impressive book offers a glimpse of Disney Magic I'm sure even Walt would appreciate.**"**

Mike Vance
"Dean of Creative Thinking"

"When it comes to turning customers into partners, nobody does it better than Disney. Connellan's format of combining useful business advice with virtually unknown Disney 'factoids' provides lots of surprises and valuable insights. It's the only business book ever written that will make you a hero to your children and traveling companions**"**

Chip R. Bell
Author of *Customers As Partners*

"I've read dozens of books on customer loyalty but this one sets the standard. It captures your attention, generates out-of-the-box thinking, and has bottom-line payoffs. The Epcot example in Chapter 13 alone is worth the price of the book. Buy it and read it!**"**

Gerald F. O'Connell
President
SCT–Manufacturing and Distribution Systems

INSIDE

THE

Magic
Kingdom

SEVEN KEYS TO DISNEY'S SUCCESS

Tom Connellan

Bard
Press

INSIDE THE MAGIC KINGDOM
Seven Keys to Disney's Success

Copyright © 1996, 1997 by Thomas K. Connellan, Ph.D.

Printed in the United States of America

ISBN 1-885167-23-7 (hardcover)

Library of Congress Cataloging-in-Publication Data

Connellan, Thomas K., date.
    Inside the Magic Kingdom : seven keys to Disney's success /
    Thomas K. Connellan.
        p.   cm.
    Includes bibliographical references.
    ISBN 1-885167-23-7 (hc)
        1. Walt Disney Company.   2. Walt Disney Company—
    Management.   I. Title.
    PN1999.W27C66   1997
    384.8'09794'94—dc21   97-780

First printing, April 1997
Second printing, October 1998
Third printing, April 1999
Fourth printing, August 1999
Fifth printing, December 1999

To Walt Disney . . .

The quintessential example
of one who dares
to dream.

CONTENTS

◆

ABOUT THIS BOOK

◆

This book is about how to take yourself, your team, and your company to the next level of customer satisfaction. One of the best ways to do that is with a good model. And Disney is one of the best models there is—especially the Magic Kingdom.

The role of Disney and the Magic Kingdom in this book is everything—and nothing.

Everything, because I've used examples of specific ways Disney people go above and beyond to enchant and hold their "guests"—as they call their customers. Most of these examples came from my extensive interviews with both current and former cast members, from senior vice presidents, to the larger-than-life characters who roam the Disney theme parks, to people behind the scenes whom you and I never see. Several other examples came from a Disney seminar I attended (details on this seminar and other programs offered by Disney are in the notes section). And a few examples came from researching the extensive literature that has been written about Disney.

To the best of my knowledge, all these specific examples in the book are true. Mary's earrings example —straight from two Disney trainers. The Epcot construction story—told to me by the individual who participated in it. The seagull-and-ice-cream anecdote— the woman it happened to is both a friend and professional colleague.

I say their role is nothing because Disney and the Magic Kingdom have not approved, disapproved, encouraged, or discouraged this book. "Mort" and the "Gang of Five" are purely fictional. They are not meant to represent any real persons, living or dead. The incidents, actions, and words ascribed to Michael Eisner in these pages are also fictional. They are my interpretation of his commitment to Disney cast members and guests and are not real events or statements. The seven key lessons are mine. They are my observations and conclusions about the factors that guide Disney's organizational behavior. So if you disagree with any of them, you're not disagreeing with anything Disney does or with any of its policies. Your disagreement is with my observations.

I hope you enjoy this book and learn from it!

OFF TO ORLANDO

Bill Greenfield stopped at the magazine kiosk outside his building and asked for a copy of *Black Enterprise*. He thought about the length of his flight to Orlando and decided to pick up copies of *Forbes* and *Fortune* as well. The latter two came to the office but wouldn't be arriving until after he left town—and Bill didn't want to wait four days to read them.

The security guard looked up as Bill entered the lobby. "Morning, Mr. Greenfield," he said. "Kind of early today, huh?"

"Early flight," Bill explained. "My wife dropped me off on her way to the office and the taxi will be here in about forty minutes. Give me a call when you see it, will you?"

1

He left the elevator, walked down the corridor to his office, and went inside. He added *American Banker* to his stack of reading material and then left an assortment of e-mail and voice mail messages for his colleagues. He began each memo with "As you know, I will be away from the office for three days and. . . ."

He leaned back in his chair and laughed to himself. He was going to Disney World, but it sounded so serious.

It was a business trip though—something that seemed best described as a curious combination of a best practices, benchmarking, and training program. Three days of learning how Disney maintained such a high level of loyalty among its guests. And anything that helped his bank increase its customer loyalty was music to Bill's ears. With the blurring of lines between banks, brokerage firms, and insurance companies, the leaders in the financial services industry were those who had replaced customer acquisition with customer retention as their dominant strategy. Bill and others knew that customer retention was becoming more and more crucial in their increasingly competitive world.

Certainly entertainment was a competitive business. And Disney had the reputation of being a company that was not necessarily easy to work with in a business-to-business relationship. Disney people were considered tough negotiators, fierce competitors, and sticklers for doing it their way.

Yet that tough business approach stood in complete contrast to Disney's treatment of its customers. People loved the parks, the movies, the paraphernalia. And that curious combination of being tough in business-to-business interactions and warm with customers seemed to pay off in the marketplace. Bill had bought Disney stock near its low in 1985 and seen it rise to almost twenty times his purchase price. He reflected on that and other things that had gone well in his life. Solid education at Howard. Great family. Vice president at a leading bank. Steady career progress.

But the phone rang, breaking his reverie.

It was the security guard. "Cab's here."

"Have fun, Mom."

"Yeah, have fun."

Carmen Rivera blew kisses at her daughters as they pressed their faces against the school bus window. She watched as the bus pulled away. Then she went back to her car and drove to the office. As she pulled into a parking space, there was Marge, one of her sales reps, trying to open the door while balancing a bag, a briefcase, and several product catalogs. "I'll help you, Marge—hold on for thirty seconds."

"I thought you were off to Disney World," said Marge.

"Plane leaves in two hours," Carmen told her.

"Sounds like fun!"

"Don't I wish!"

She was going to learn about Disney's customer service methods, something her own company really needed to know more about. The whole health-care industry was going through major changes, and the opportunities for those with superior products and services—like those Carmen's company offered—were enormous. Carmen knew that any major change creates opportunities for someone to capitalize on that shift. And Carmen intended to use the Disney visit as a springboard to do just that.

She still wondered what both her sales team and the other members of the management team thought. Oh, she'd met formally with each group yesterday, but she wanted a more spontaneous response.

"Marge," she said. "Sit down with me for a minute. I'd like your input on something."

Don Jenkins sat staring out the window at the edge of the wing and the tarmac beyond. He hated spending time in planes. Come to think of it, he hated everything about this trip, a total waste of time if you asked him.

What was he supposed to learn from Mickey Mouse and Goofy? He pulled out the hotel information and Walt Disney World map. Mickey beamed out at him from the cover of the map.

"Oh, Disney World!" the flight attendant chirped. "Your first trip?"

He looked up at her and scowled. "First," he said, "and last."

Judy Crawford ran her hand through her hair, watching the weather map on the monitor. "Oh, no," she wailed. "I don't see how I can get out of here with all this going on."

She was talking about the major storm that had cut through the Southeast just hours ago. It was playing havoc with electrical service to businesses and homes throughout the region. Indeed, Judy's banks of phones hadn't stopped ringing for hours.

"We can handle it, Judy," her assistant told her. "Isn't that right?" he asked the others in the room, and even though they were all engrossed in taking phone calls, they looked up and either nodded or gave a thumbs-up. Judy smiled. She'd trained them well and they did a bang-up job. Still, shouldn't she be here with them in a situation like this and not off at the Magic Kingdom? Oh, of course, she'd been absolutely thrilled about the chance to go back there. She'd always promised herself that she would. And it wasn't as though it would be all fun and games, because the training program promised to give her an inside look at the way Disney provided the extraordinary service that it did.

And wasn't service what Judy was all about?

She reached for the phone, but her assistant grabbed it first. He spoke softly into the mouthpiece, then covered it and said one word to her: "Go."

Alan Zimmerman looked in the mirror and thanked the barber for the quick trim. It hadn't been absolutely necessary, but he had a meeting down on Sand Hill Road early his first morning back and wanted to be ready for that. Alan paid the barber and headed back into the airport proper to see if a new departure time had been posted.

Alan looked younger than his thirty-eight years, something that he hoped would turn into an advantage by the time he was fifty-eight. Right now it was mostly a source of good-natured ribbing from his fellow members of the Young Presidents Organization. He enjoyed a close relationship with the other people in his chapter. In fact, it was one of them who told him about this Disney thing.

At first, he had been skeptical. Disney? He knew Disney had dramatically moved up the Fortune 500 list the last few years and they were near the top of *Fortune*'s most admired companies. But what could he learn at Disney that could be applied to his own software firm? The friend who had buttonholed him was pretty persuasive, pointing out that, for a software firm, each 1 percent increase in customer retention equaled a 7 percent increase in profits. Persuaded by those numbers—and the fact that 70 percent of all visitors to Disney World are repeat visitors—Alan signed up.

FIVE AT THE STARTING GATE

Day 1, 9:30–10:00 A.M.

Carmen Rivera watched the people walking past City Hall, intent on finding those with the name tags like hers. The crowds streamed by. Carmen had heard that some 33 million people a year visited Disney's three Florida theme parks. And it felt like all of them were there today.

For most people, Disney World was a playground, but for Carmen it was business. Well, mostly business—after all, it was the biggest theme park in the hemisphere. Vice president of sales at a leading distributor of health-care products, she welcomed this opportunity to see how Disney wowed its visitors. She had learned from a networking friend about this special opportunity—a walking tour of Walt Disney World, guided by Mort

Vandeleur, a former cast member at both Disneyland and Disney World who now helped other companies improve their customer focus. Besides, it was Disney World—a place she had visited once before and wanted to visit again.

Carmen was proud of her record. Fueled by her single-minded focus and determination, Carmen's company—a firm other distributors referred to when using the term "best practices"—was enjoying strong double-digit growth. She and her team were proud of what they had created, but Carmen, never content with less than perfection, had privately determined to find ways to increase customer loyalty.

Carmen had worked her way up through the sales ranks with her knack for building good customer relationships. She had a well-honed business sense and a way of dealing fairly with salespeople that made her one of the company's most widely respected managers. At the same time, she promoted company profitability— like the time she was able to suggest process changes at the inside order desk that reduced cycle time on orders by six hours and cut days of sales outstanding by one day.

Mort had called to welcome her the previous afternoon, shortly after she had arrived at her hotel. She had been impressed by his enthusiasm, his apparently genuine eagerness to meet her. "We'll meet at 10:00 just in front of City Hall," he had said. "It's to the left after you enter the Magic Kingdom. And if you see four other people with name tags looking lost, introduce yourself.

They're the other members of our little gang." Mort's voice was warm and friendly, Carmen noted. He'd even made her smile at the way he'd used the word "gang."

From a few steps away, Bill Greenfield saw Carmen standing alone. Even from the side, he could see that she was not there just to have fun. She was looking intently at the faces of the people who were gathering, as if trying to read their thoughts.

When she turned toward him, Bill saw that she was wearing the distinctive name tag Mort had sent. He walked faster, pointing at his own tag as he approached.

Carmen looked at his tag and smiled, her deep brown eyes lighting up. "Hello, Bill," she said. "I see you're also here for Mort's session."

Bill noted her slacks, her colorful, hand-painted T-shirt, and her sneakers. He was instantly sorry he had worn his suit. It was a habit that was hard to break, the natural reserve and deep-voiced dignity that he'd cultivated throughout his career.

She's twenty years younger than I am, at least, he thought, letting himself off the hook for his formality. *People dress more casually nowadays.* But then he heard his wife's voice as he was packing: "It's Disney World, Bill. Take some polo shirts. Take some slacks."

Six foot three and still fit at fifty-eight years of age, he was a commercial loan officer at a bank in the Northwest. Now he was working on a special team charged with looking at how other organizations kept a constant focus on their customers.

Although he had some doubts about whether or not he would be spending time frivolously, he had decided to learn as much as he could—after all, Disney's stock performance and financial success were not only well known but would have been the envy of any company.

Bill's bank knew the impact that customer loyalty could have on profitability—they had just finished a study on the relationship between customer retention and profitability, which showed that every 1 percent increase in customer retention produced $1.5 million in increased profits. Bill's reading of similar studies found that comparable improvements occurred not only in other financial service firms but also other industries.

Not least, he was becoming uncomfortable with the thought that all work and no play might be making him a dull guy, as his wife playfully called him the last time the grandchildren had come to visit. "You've got to make things fun for them," she'd said.

Well, maybe he'd learn something like that here, where fun *was* the business.

Carmen shook his hand. "I think there are three more of us, plus Mort," she said. "I'm ready to get moving, aren't you?" She scanned the crowd again. "I wonder what Mort looks like."

"He told me he'd be wearing a yellow shirt," said Bill.

"Yes, but I keep expecting to see white gloves and red shorts with big yellow buttons," she grinned.

"And big ears?" He found himself grinning back.

"Exactly."

"I think I've seen him in the movies," he said, laughing.

"**H**i!" said a lively voice behind them. "Are you two looking for Mort?"

They turned and saw a pixieish young woman with short red hair who could have been one of this year's high school graduates. "I'm Judy," she said. Then she indicated a tanned, slender man of about forty who was standing behind her. "And this is Alan."

Alan held out his hand. "I guess we're all here for the same reason," he said.

"We're part of—what does Mort call us? His little gang," Judy said.

"The Gang of Five," Carmen offered.

"Then one of us is still missing," Bill noted.

"And Mort's missing, too," Judy reminded them.

Judy Crawford was, at twenty-eight, one of the youngest team leaders in her company, a regional electric utility based in North Carolina. An unfailingly cheerful person, she had been a natural leader of the customer relations team from her first day on the job three years ago. Her positive outlook on life was already legendary. Her team members continually tested her— sometimes playfully, sometimes inadvertently—but had never seen her angry. When spring storms blew in and lightning danced, hundreds of customers would call to complain bitterly about power outages; she usually left them happily thanking her for the crew who would soon arrive to restore their electricity.

When the opportunity came to explore best practices at Disney, Judy jumped at it. She knew it would be a good way to make her department even better at handling customers. She knew because she had been to Walt Disney World three times already—once in high school, once on her honeymoon, and once with her husband and four-year-old daughter. Who could be better at customer relations than an organization that averaged 50–75,000 guests a day, nearly all of whom left happy?

> **" *Just when everyone is saying how great you are is when you're the most vulnerable.* "**

Judy had run into Alan Zimmerman in the coffee shop of her hotel that morning. Alan was an outgoing, energetic man who had played varsity baseball while operating a small landscaping business to put himself through college. He knew of Disney's great success at service quality and had decided this would be an excellent opportunity to discover ways to increase customer loyalty to his fast-growing, California-based software company.

Not that his company wasn't doing well. It was. He delighted in hearing the accolades, reading the comments on their success in the trade press, being interviewed in the local papers. Then he'd run across a quote by Walt Disney. He had paraphrased the quote and now carried it on the back of a business card in his wallet: "Just when everyone is saying how great you are is when you're the most vulnerable." The "Red Zone," Walt had called it. Alan figured he was in the Red Zone and was determined to avoid its dangers.

He had not, however, expected to start his discovery experience by actually exploring the Magic Kingdom. He felt a little guilty. How would he explain this to his two boys? He'd certainly have to make it up to them with another trip. There was no way around it.

He pointed to the castle in the distance. "Doesn't really seem as though we're going to work, does it?"

J ust then, a tall, trim man with silver hair and mustache, wearing a short-sleeved, yellow knit shirt, strode up and announced, "Hello! I'm Mort!" He was confident, obviously used to talking to strangers, putting them at ease. "I count four, so we're missing one. Has our fifth been waylaid somewhere?" he asked as he shook their hands.

"I'm here," said a dour-looking, square-rigged, fortyish, dark-haired man in gray slacks and an open-necked white sport shirt. He'd had his back turned to the group, and so had gone unnoticed as he stooped to clean his shoe with a napkin. "Give me a minute. I just stepped in some kid's gum."

Don Jenkins was not happy to be here. As a trained engineer and site manager for a large auto supply manufacturer, he had better ways to use his time and had said so to his group vice president. He pointed out that his lean-manufacturing initiative had lowered inventory levels, cut cycle time, and improved productivity—and he had the numbers to prove it. The boss said he knew Don was a sharp man with a pencil, doing a great job, but wanted him to go anyway, to find a way to "raise the bar"—to take customer satisfaction to the next level.

So Don had wedged his solidly built frame into a coach-class seat on a direct flight from Chicago to Orlando—which had departed, he noted, more than ten minutes behind schedule and arrived twelve minutes late—and prepared himself to waste several perfectly good days mingling with Mickey, Goofy, and the Seven Dwarfs. Even so, he was determined to salvage as much productive time as possible. He had already placed six calls on his cell phone before running afoul of the kid's bubble gum.

He glanced at his watch now, out of habit, and didn't even bother to greet Carmen, Judy, Alan, or Bill.

"Here's the plan," said Mort. "I've identified seven keys that contribute to Disney's success. Over the next three days, we will walk, talk, and observe what goes on in the Magic Kingdom. From the keys, you'll learn seven lessons that you can apply in your organization to make it as successful as Disney.

"We'll start by having breakfast at the bakery on Main Street. Has anybody not eaten this morning?" Carmen raised her hand. "Well, you're in luck, Carmen. Our first stop will be for something to eat. We'll sit and have some coffee or orange juice, get to know one another a little better, and talk about what we'll do for the rest of the day.

"Now, before we enjoy a late breakfast, are there any questions that need answering immediately?"

No one spoke. Don watched a jet taking off in the distance, heading north. Mort was too smooth. He was already getting on Don's nerves.

"Well, then," said Mort, "I've got one question that you can be thinking about. Who should Disney consider their competition? Who do people compare Disney World with? That's a question few people ask me, because the answer seems so obvious." He studied their faces.

"Think about that while we head over to the bakery."

WHO'S REALLY YOUR COMPETITION?

Day 1, 10:00–11:00 A.M.

As they sipped their coffee over bagels and donuts, Judy and Alan chatted about their kids, and Bill and Carmen compared notes on their businesses. Don sat at the far end of the table staring into his appointment book as if it were the most interesting thing in the room.

Carmen turned to Mort. "All right, I give up. Who are Disney World's competitors? Other theme or amusement parks, of course, but that's obvious. Besides, I'm not really sure you could call it competition. People go to other parks, like Universal Studios or Six Flags, but doesn't that usually just whet their appetite? It's like movies—going to one doesn't keep you from going to others."

17

Alan said, "Actually, in a way, anyone who goes after discretionary dollars could be considered a competitor. So the competition could include movies, athletic events, and things like that."

Mort smiled. "It's actually broader than that. In a very real sense, Disney has hundreds of competitors. Thousands, really. L. L. Bean, FedEx, and GE are some of the top competitors."

Four puzzled faces looked at him; Don frowned and looked out the window.

"Then I'm not sure what you mean when you say competitor," said Carmen. "None of those are theme parks, or even close."

"I'll go one step further," said Mort. "Not only does Disney regard them as competition, but so should you."

Alan's brow furrowed. "I don't see your point. We're a software company. None of the companies you named develops software—at least, as far as I know."

Mort turned to the person on the other side of him. "Carmen, how about you? Do you regard any of those companies as your competition?"

Carmen hesitated. "Well, we sell some advanced biofunction monitors that are used in operating rooms and in aerospace, so I guess GE might be considered a competitor."

Bill and Judy sat quietly, a quizzical look on their faces. Bill thought, *How could any of those companies be in competition with a bank?* Carmen was wondering if they had subsidiaries she was unaware of.

"I think maybe I see where you're going with this," said Judy.

Don squirmed a little, propped his chin on his fist, and stared out the window. *Here we go again,* he thought. *Another new business theory. More spaced-out New Age nonsense about the New World Order and global competition. More ways to waste productive work time.* He drummed the tips of his fingers on the surface of the table.

A half-hour into it, and the unrelieved cheerfulness of the place was already beginning to grate on him. The waiters, the cashiers, the maintenance people—didn't anyone wake up grumpy in this world? He smiled grimly at his own Seven Dwarfs pun. This place was getting to him, though not the way his boss had hoped.

Maybe the others could see the point of this pointless exercise, but he couldn't. After all, numbers were what counted. If something existed, it existed in quantity. If it existed in quantity, there was a number for it. If there wasn't a number for something, it didn't exist.

Product quality was what beating the competition was all about. Design fool-proof production methods, implement them carefully, monitor each process carefully, and continuously improve methods.

Why did his VP want him to attend this nonsense, anyway? The guy was a numbers man, like Don. And yet. . . . Lately he'd been making noises about unhappy customers. Don wasn't worried; a good product would always sell itself. Let the marketing guys worry about customer loyalty.

Outside the window he saw a little girl with curly red hair, wearing Mickey Mouse glasses and a too-big Goofy hat. Her hands were smudged with chocolate, dirt, and tears, and she was distressed about something. Her mother was trying to comfort her. *So,* he thought, *not everyone here is hap-hap-happy after all.*

Carmen saw it, too. She leaned toward the window instinctively, as if to comfort the child.

Mort silently observed their reactions. He also saw something they didn't. The girl's father was talking to a Disney employee, someone wearing a Disney badge. He smiled. Perhaps he could use this later, when he talked about paying attention to details.

Mort liked details, collected them like colorful postage stamps. He had studied the information these five had sent him about their experience, their education, their companies—everything they felt comfortable sharing with him. He knew their areas of expertise—software, health care, auto parts, utilities, banking—so he could make a pretty good guess at who they thought they were in competition with.

He turned to Judy. "Tell me, then: How is L. L. Bean your competitor?"

"Well, it has to do with just plain old customer satisfaction, doesn't it?"

"Exactly," Mort said. "Your competition is anyone who raises customer expectations—because if someone else satisfies customers better than you, no matter what type of business, you suffer by comparison." The others nodded. Except Don, of course.

"One of the ways people experience the Magic Kingdom is by telephone," Mort went on. "Disney gets thousands of calls every day. Many of them are the same people who also call FedEx and count on their responsiveness and reliability. Maybe they call just before or just after, or maybe a week earlier or a week later. But they do call.

"Then they go home at night and order something from L. L. Bean. Or maybe they're one of the several hundred thousand people who call the GE answer center every year. Do they compare those phone calls? You bet they do! Either consciously or unconsciously, people compare every one of those phone calls.

"Carmen, I assume your products get delivered to your customers—and what I'm saying is that your customers compare your delivery reliability to that of FedEx, as well as every other delivery firm they use.

❝ *If someone else satisfies customers better than you, no matter what type of business, you suffer by comparison.* ❞

"You see, people judge not only their overall experience but also what happens transaction by transaction. They compare phone call to phone call, invoice to invoice, check-in to check-in, delivery to delivery."

Mort leaned toward the group and spoke in a quiet but firm voice. "And this simple fact is causing a fundamental change in the way competition takes place. Competition is no longer the bank across town or the auto dealer down the street or the distributor in the next county. The 'competition' is literally anyone customers come in contact with that they compare you to. So what Judy said is right. Everyone's competing in the field of customer satisfaction. I suspect she knows that because she's had to deal with thousands of customers on the phone."

"You're sure right about that," said Judy, her eyes sparkling as she remembered some of those folks. She could sure tell Mort some stories!

But Alan, thinking about his software company, spoke first. "Mort," he asked, "are you saying that Disney World and my company are, in effect, competitors?"

Mort smiled, expecting a response like this. "Don't know," he answered. "Do you ever do business with people who've been guests here?"

"I'd guess that half or more of our customers have been here," Alan said. "Maybe three-fourths."

"Well, for that 75 percent of your customers, sure, we're a form of competition."

"And the other 25 percent?"

"Only if they've ever talked to someone who's been here."

Alan laughed. "That's what I was afraid you'd say." He shook his head. "Everyone. Everyone's our competition."

"Sort of puts a different light on things, doesn't it?" asked Mort, smiling.

"Sure does," said Alan. "Makes you rethink how you do business." The others—all except Don—nodded agreement, intrigued at this novel idea about their customers.

"Then what about internal customers?" asked Judy. "Does this apply to our dealings with them?"

"Sure," said Mort. "Internal customers look for the same things as external customers. When an internal customer calls you, he compares your phone response to the response he gets at L. L. Bean or FedEx.

"Now, everybody finished?" Mort surveyed their progress. "Let's take a stroll down Main Street. But, as a reminder, here's the first key lesson to Disney's success." He handed each of them a small card, on which was printed the following:

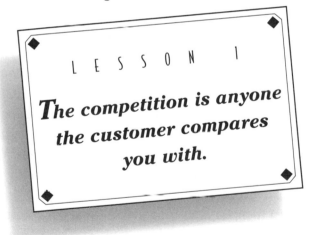

L E S S O N 1

The competition is anyone the customer compares you with.

As they left the restaurant, Don read his card, turned it over, shrugged, and stuck it into his pocket. *Maybe the guy has a point,* he thought. *But a couple of phone calls do not a business make. Lots more to it than that.*

The six of them walked down Main Street, Bill and Carmen out front, Don bringing up the rear. Judy and Mort were chatting casually with Alan. Bill watched Disney World guests wandering happily from store to store, up and down the street, heading off toward the attractions in other parts of the park. He saw park employees—cast members, Mort called them—busily playing the parts of shop owners, moving and dusting furniture, sweeping the walk, working at food carts, apparently enjoying the experience as much as the people they were serving. What was it that kept them so happy? And was happy the same as being committed?

> " *Internal customers look for the same things as external customers. They compare your response to L. L. Bean or FedEx.* "

Just then, Carmen nudged Bill. "That may be one of the reasons it's always so clean here," she said. "See that guy? He doesn't look like a custodian, but he just walked twenty feet out of his way, picked up a piece of paper, and backtracked to put it in a trash can. Do you suppose they economize on their custodial staff?"

Mort overheard, and called out, "Ask him."

"I think I will," said Bill. He approached the man, who had stopped to talk with another cast member. "Excuse me, sir," Bill began. The man turned to meet Bill's gaze with intense blue eyes. "Are you part of the custodial staff?"

A noisy group of guests all but surrounded them, making it difficult to hear. "Yes, I am," said the man above their raucous laughter. He and Mort exchanged a quick glance.

"That's interesting. Thanks. I'm sorry I interrupted you," said Bill. He turned and started back. Halfway there he stopped, turned, and called out, "How many people are on the custodial staff?"

The man attempted to shout over the noise of the crowd. Bill thought he answered, "Forty-five thousand," but that couldn't be right. Bill started to ask again, but the man was already moving away.

When Bill rejoined the group, he told Carmen, "Apparently the guy really is a custodian. He said there are four to five thousand, if I heard right."

"That's a lot!" said Carmen.

"Lots of kids dropping their gum, spilling ice cream, that kind of thing," said Don. Bill and Carmen smiled politely.

Alan, doing a little mental arithmetic, agreed that four to five thousand did seem like an unwieldy custodial crew. Judy, on the other hand, was enthralled. "No wonder it's so neat and tidy here!"

Mort had silently watched the whole thing. Should he straighten it out? Better to wait until the right time. Let the situation clarify itself. Maybe he could even help it along a little.

HOW LITTLE THINGS MAKE A BIG DIFFERENCE

Day 1, 1:30–3:00 P.M.

Later in the day, after a general tour through Frontierland, Adventureland, and Liberty Square, the Gang of Five returned to Main Street with their leader. Mort gathered the group around him and put his hand on one of the horse-head hitching posts that lined the street. "Nice, aren't they?"

Everyone looked at the hitching posts. Yes, they were interesting, well designed, well made, clean, shiny, appropriate for the place—everything a hitching post should be in a fanciful replica of an old-fashioned American main street. But aside from that—what?

So they looked at the hitching posts, looked back to Mort, and smiled wanly. "Uh-huh, nice, very nice," they agreed. Then they waited.

Alan broke the brief silence. "We're supposed to ask you something about the hitching posts, right?"

Mort laughed. "If you would."

"Okay. What's the significance of the hitching posts?"

"I was hoping you'd ask that. It has to do with the second key I want to offer you." He handed everyone another card:

L E S S O N 2

Pay fantastic attention to detail.

"You see, the high wear points on these horse-head hitching posts are stripped down and repainted every night."

They all looked at each other.

"Every single hitching post every single night?" Judy asked.

"If that's what's needed, then yes," said Mort. "But it's not always necessary. The goal is to have the park looking fresh every morning. There are thirty-seven hitching posts here. They don't all get the same wear, but the high-wear points are done every night."

Bill raised an eyebrow. Judy grinned at Mort. "Now, Mort, you wouldn't be pulling our leg, would you?" she said.

Mort shook his head no.

Don looked exasperated. "You know," he said, "I appreciate attention to detail as much as the next guy. In fact, I'm considered the detail fanatic in my company. But repainting these things every night seems to me a waste of resources. Why not spend the money and effort where it's needed? And if there has to be a regular schedule, why not once a week, or once a month? You could probably get by with doing it every three or four months. Your customers have other things on their minds. How many of them will notice the difference?" He looked around at the others.

"It's worse than you think, Don," said Mort. "Not only are the hitching posts repainted every night, the starting time is based on the temperature and humidity, so the paint will be dry by the time the park opens the next morning."

Judy gave a short whistle; Don just shook his head.

Mort continued, emphasizing his words: "A company that will pay that amount of attention to a hitching post will pay that much attention to anything that comes in contact with its guests, because attention to detail is part of the company's culture. Now, I'd like for you to answer this question for yourself." He looked at each of them in turn. "Is that same level of attention to detail part of your company's culture?"

All were silent. Bill thought about the time a customer had buttonholed him in the lobby to ask for a deposit slip; there were none left on the customer service counter, and no one on the staff seemed to know whose responsibility it was to keep them supplied. A small detail, but how many times had it caused a customer to begin thinking that this couldn't-care-less attitude extended to all the bank's operations, even to accounting and security?

Others had similar thoughts. Alan ran his hand over one of the hitching posts. "If I translate that into the way we deal with our customers," he said, "I'm appalled at some of the things that have happened. In my company, I have always emphasized total commitment to customer satisfaction, but one time. . . . Well, let's put it this way: We're good, but we're not this good."

Carmen knew that although attention to detail was critical in manufacturing the high quality health-care products she and her team sold, it was also crucial in distributing and selling them, as well as in making sure the company's products were used correctly. In her job, attention to detail was not only a matter of creating and keeping customers; it could mean the difference between life and death. She remembered the time she'd insisted on rewording one of their package inserts until there was no way the instructions could be misunderstood. But the design staff had complained mightily. . . .

As far as I'm concerned, she thought, *we've still got a long way to go.*

"I'd be willing to bet nobody does it like Disney," said Judy. "But can you give us some other examples?"

"Sure," said Mort. "This place is full of them. Follow me."

The great castle loomed before them. Mort led the group to up to the main entrance. Inside, he came quickly to a large mural on the wall.

"Look over here," said Mort, waving his arm. They turned and looked. To their right was a huge mural illustrating scenes from *Cinderella.* "Pretty nice, huh?"

"Beautiful!" said Judy. Bill and Alan nodded.

"There are a number of reasons why this is a good example of attention to detail," said Mort. "But they may not be obvious at first. See if you can find one."

They studied the mural in silence. Then Carmen said, "Oh, I think I see one. It's been a while since I read *Cinderella,* but I remember that one of the stepsisters was 'green with envy' and the other was 'red with rage.' And there they are! That's exactly how the artist painted them! Their cheeks are tinted red with rage and green with envy."

"Ooooh!" said Judy. "You're right! I've been here a thousand times—well, three, anyway—and I never noticed that!"

"Most people don't," said Mort. "But the point is, you just did. Some people will see these details right away. Others will see them after several visits, and it will make their visit just a little bit richer. People come here for a variety of reasons—they like to visit a particular attraction, they enjoy the atmosphere of the place, they want to revisit their childhood. If there's something new to discover every time they visit, they're more inclined to come back again. For some it's a new ride or attraction, but for many others it's something in the details they never saw before. The people at Disney World think that's important, and that's why they pay attention to the smallest details.

> **❝ *Ask yourself:*
> *Is Disney-like attention*
> *to detail part of*
> *your company's*
> *culture?* ❞**

"Another example of this attention to detail is the way the castle is constructed. The stones near the bottom are larger than those near the top. It makes the castle appear bigger without making it too imposing.

"The same technique is used in other parts of the park. In the Haunted Mansion, for example. On Main Street, if you compare the second stories with the first stories, you'll see that the second stories are smaller. And the third stories are smaller than the second stories. Probably the clearest example of this is the

Crystal Arts store because the third-story windows are lined up exactly over the second-story windows. And even though it's a three-story building, it's only slightly taller than the two-story building next door.

"Now, I know some of you will continue to have doubts about whether it's worthwhile to focus so much attention on every detail. You may have found it most profitable, perhaps even essential, to prioritize or ration your resources. Disney does the same thing. No one has unlimited resources. But Disney puts its resources into anything that affects the guests' experience in either the short term or long term.

"This is the Magic Kingdom. And if it's going to stay magic, we have to continue to pay close attention to every detail.

"My question to you is this: If you knew that increased attention to some detail would improve customer loyalty, how much more attention would you be willing to focus on it?"

As they walked back toward Main Street, Bill spoke. "I'm curious about who takes care of all the details. It seems like an enormous undertaking—how do they even decide which details to focus on?"

"It starts with a process called 'Imagineering,'" Mort began, "by people who are called 'Imagineers.' They begin their planning process with something called 'the sky's the limit' sessions."

"Imagine studying to be an Imagineer," Judy giggled.

Mort laughed along with the others, but went on. "The Imagineers start by deciding on a big concept. They might decide, 'Okay, we're going to build a water park.' Then they brainstorm the concept—generate all the possibilities they can think of. I know that when they were working on the water park idea, at one point they considered creating a military camp gone haywire. But out of all the ideas they generated, the best one they came up with was a typhoon. That's how we got Typhoon Lagoon. But pretty much everything starts in Imagineering."

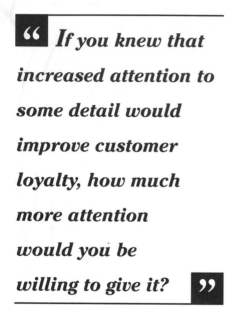

❝ *If you knew that increased attention to some detail would improve customer loyalty, how much more attention would you be willing to give it?* ❞

"So they come up with possibilities, pick the best one, design the pieces, and then it's built?"

"In a nutshell, Bill, that's pretty much the way it happens," Mort told him. "But there is fanatical attention to detail starting way back in the planning process. For instance, before anything is built, they plan the colors."

"Colors?" Don said.

"Colors. John Hench does all the colors. He was one of the nine original artists—he's in his eighties now—and he's the color guy for everything: Paris, Tokyo, Epcot. Hotels, too. He designs the color scheme for each hotel.

"He even does the color schemes for the walkways, taking into account details like where the sun is going to fall at different times of the year. He designed the night lighting of Epcot's big orb to maintain just the right purple hue. Attention to detail permeates everything."

"So it's not just the Magic Kingdom, but Epcot, too?" asked Judy.

"Everything. Each attraction, each hotel, each shop, everything gets that same attention to detail."

Mort stopped and thought for a moment. "You're staying at the Polynesian, right? I'll give you an example of what I mean. Let's hop the monorail for a quick trip over to your hotel."

When they reached the Polynesian Hotel, Mort and the Gang of Five strode through the lobby and out onto the beach. Mort waved his hand in a complete circle from the Seven Seas Lagoon past a wing of the hotel, past the swimming pool, and back to the Seven Seas Lagoon. "Now, keeping in mind that we're looking for attention to detail, what do you see here that illustrates the principle?"

Everyone looked around silently for a few moments. Then Alan said, "I worked my way through college doing landscaping, and I spent part of my military service in the South Pacific—and two things are apparent to me.

"First, the vegetation here and on those islands makes it look as though we are actually in Polynesia. I don't know for sure that all the vegetation is actually indigenous to Polynesia, but at first glance, it sure looks that way.

"Second," he said, "it seems to me that a lot of detailed planning has gone into the landscape. It appears to be random growth, but the only thing I can see are the tops of three structures in the Magic Kingdom and virtually nothing as I look back toward the hotel. That suggests that the height, density, location, and type of vegetation was carefully thought out. Very carefully."

"Right on both counts," said Mort approvingly. "The vegetation is a mixture of Polynesian plants and native vegetation that closely resembles the real thing."

"It's not just the Polynesian," said Carmen. "Last year, my family and I stayed at Wilderness Lodge here in Disney World. It actually felt like the Rockies. They hid the lodge away from everything—tucked away out on the point. It looks like it's built of logs. There are moose tracks and bear tracks all over the place. There's less direct sunlight there than almost anywhere else in the park. It feels cool, like you're deep in the forest. You could almost believe you're somewhere out in the wilderness. Same thing with the vegetation. I'm sure you wouldn't find most of it growing naturally in Florida, although it feels perfectly natural in that location."

She smiled, remembering the visit with pleasure, then went on. "There's a big stone fireplace, seven or eight stories tall. When I asked someone about it, I was told it was based on the rock layers in the Grand Canyon. Sure enough, when we went to each floor we could read about the geologic period represented by that layer. So it not only felt right, it was educational. My kids were fascinated. When we got home, they went to the library and checked out books on geology.

"Everything is in keeping with the rustic feel of the place—right down to the numbers on the doors to the rooms. The designers researched about thirty different lodges around the West. One of them was this place near the Grand Canyon called the Thunderbird. They liked how the Thunderbird numbered its doors, so they adapted that design for the Wilderness Lodge.

"Something else," she continued. "When I went behind the lodge, I couldn't see anything except Discovery Island. I know the Contemporary area is nearby, but you can't see it. You can't see anything that's not wilderness.

"It's like here at the Polynesian. When you're here, you're in Polynesia and nowhere else. There, you're in one of our national park hotels, like Old Faithful Inn in Yellowstone.

"Except for one thing." She added. "Or maybe I should say twelve things. Twelve things that don't really have anything to do with wilderness or our national parks. Twelve things my kids found out about, hidden in plain sight, so to speak. There are twelve—"

Mort interrupted her with a sharp whistle. Carmen fell silent, and she and the others looked at him curiously. He put a finger to his lips. "Hold that thought, Carmen," he said. Then he smiled. "I'll see all of you in the morning in front of City Hall at 9:00."

Don pulled his notebook from his pocket and wrote something in it, while the others, mystified, watched Mort's departure.

MICHAEL EISNER SETS THE RECORD STRAIGHT

Day 2, 8:50 A.M.–1:30 P.M.

Mort liked to arrive early and watch the park come to life. But someone else apparently had the same idea. When he got to City Hall at ten till nine, he found Judy already there, chatting with a cast member. Alan, Bill, and Carmen joined them soon after, followed by an expressionless Don, who walked up on the stroke of nine with a studiously casual air, saying nothing.

Over a light breakfast, the Gang of Five reviewed the previous day's lessons. As they talked, Mort glanced out the window and noticed a family looking at a map, holding it first this way, then that. Excusing himself from the group, he went outside and began talking with them. At one point, he bent down and said something to one of the children. The little girl, who appeared to be about ten years old, broke out in a big smile. Mort pointed—an odd, two-fingered point, Don noticed—and the family looked off in the direction indicated, nodded, and seemed grateful for his help.

"What was going on there?" asked Alan when Mort returned.

"What I was just doing was being 'aggressively friendly,'" Mort explained. "All cast members are strongly urged to stop whatever they're doing, if they can, and offer help whenever they see a guest in need. That's the official term for a visitor—a 'guest.' If they see guests puzzling over a map, they offer help. If someone's trying to take a group photo, they offer to take the picture so everyone can be in the shot.

"Being aggressively friendly also happens to be a good example of this morning's topic." Mort handed everyone a card with the following words printed on it:

L E S S O N   3

*Everyone walks
the talk.*

Don read his card and rolled his eyes, tucking the card into his pocket.

Bill studied the message for a minute, then asked, "If you were an employee—excuse me, *cast member*—then what you just did would be part of your job. Is that what 'walking the talk' amounts to—doing your job?"

"No," Mort said. "The point of the lesson is more about the *way* you do your job. The Magic Kingdom is about fun and magic. As you come in on the monorail, the announcer says, 'You're about to arrive at the most magical place in the world.' Every cast member wants to preserve that magical experience. Every one of them wants to help guests enjoy their visit to the fullest extent possible. They don't just talk about it. That would be 'talking the talk.' They do it. That's 'walking the talk.' Guests will average sixty contact opportunities—points where they come in contact with a cast member. Disney wants to make each of those a magic moment. Cast members actively seek out the opportunity to create one of those magic moments.

"So when the opportunity arises, everyone proactively helps the guest. I helped that family with some directions because that's what was needed for them to enjoy their visit, and I happened to be the one who first saw that they needed that help. It could have just as easily been a custodian or anyone else, because every cast member works at being aggressively friendly.

"So when the culture says, 'Help the guest,' it applies to everyone. Every single person 'walks the talk.' Accountants walk the talk; mechanical engineers walk the talk; supervisors walk the talk. In the Magic Kingdom, everyone walks the talk."

"The culture?" Don asked.

"The way Disney World does business," Mort said. "That's what we mean by culture here."

"You know," said Judy looking thoughtful, "sometimes you say 'we' and sometimes you say 'they.' Which is it? Are you actually a cast member, Mort, or do you just feel like one?"

"It's actually a case of *feeling* like one," smiled Mort. "I don't work for Disney—haven't for a long time. I just think they do a great job, and I enjoy showing groups like yours how to take your business to the next level by learning from the best—and Disney is clearly a leader at customer focus."

"Then the five of us, as guests, or whatever we are, we could walk the talk too, couldn't we?" asked Judy playfully.

"There's nothing to stop you," said Mort. "In fact, we've been really successful in instilling this helpful attitude in all our cast members when we see how much of it rubs off on guests. People—guests and everybody— seem more friendly, more neighborly in here than they do outside the park. I'm sure some of it's because people are having a good time here at Disney, but at the same time, I can't help feeling that a lot of it comes from our cast members' attitudes.

"I've seen guests go out of their way to help someone having a hard time with a wheelchair. I've seen people comforting a lost child while others go to Guest
Relations for help in locating the parents. Sure, people
do these things on the outside, but in here it seems to
be the rule rather than the exception. I find it pretty
darned inspiring, even after all these years of studying
this place.

"Think about your own company. Every time a customer comes in contact with your company, you have
an opportunity to create value. Capitalize on that opportunity and you win. Waste it and you lose. It's as simple
as that."

Mort glanced at his wristwatch. "Okay, if you're all
finished with your coffee and bagels, there's a special
presentation I'd like you to attend, about five minutes
from here. And, frankly, because of something we wit-
nessed yesterday, I think you'll really enjoy it. I wish I
could take credit for it, but I could not have arranged a
better illustration of what we were just talking about.

"Now," he said, "are you all sufficiently intrigued?
Then follow me, please."

The Gang of Five soon found themselves in a class-
room, where about thirty other people were already
seated. Mort took a seat at the end of the front row; the
others sat nearby.

Mort turned in his chair and said, "I think you'll like this. Michael Eisner—the chairman and CEO of the Walt Disney Company—is in the park today. He's going to stop by for a few minutes to share some thoughts and answer your questions.

"Here he comes now." All eyes turned to a side door, where an energetic man in a polo shirt and Mickey Mouse ears was smiling, shaking hands, and clapping people on the shoulder as he entered the room.

He had intense blue eyes.

"Bill!" whispered Carmen. "Isn't that—"

"The custodian we saw yesterday? The one I talked to? It sure looks like him."

"It *is* him!"

"Yes, it is," said Mort. "After I saw you talk with him yesterday, Bill, I was hoping I could arrange this little surprise for you today. So—surprise! If you have any questions that need answers, now's the best time to ask them."

The rest of the people in the room were standing, applauding Eisner as he walked to the lectern. "Hello, everybody! It's great to be able to spend some time with you. Everybody got Pixie Dust?"

"Yeah!" they answered, laughing.

Eisner turned toward the Gang of Five. "Hi, Mort!" he said. "Good to see you again. Got your own class with you, I see. Welcome, folks!"

Why would a big shot like Eisner waste his time with a Mickey Mouse training class? Don thought. *Or even take two seconds to answer Bill's question yesterday?*

Eisner spoke to the class for a few minutes, then offered to answer questions. As he concluded his comments, he said, "No one ever wants to ask the first question, so who would like to ask the second question?" It got a small laugh, then the room filled with questions.

What a clever way to start questions flowing, thought Alan. Back home, when he gathered people together for a meeting, it was sometimes difficult to get them to open up. Eisner's approach, on the other hand, immediately put people at ease. Alan made a note to remember the way he did it.

> **" *Every time a customer comes in contact with your company you have an opportunity to create value.* "**

Carmen asked the question that had bothered her since the day before. "Mr. Eisner," she began, "yesterday we asked you—or someone who looked like you—a question about how many people were part of the custodial crew here. We thought you said four to five thousand. I have two questions. One, was that really you yesterday? And two, that seems like a very large number of people for custodial staff, even though I must admit this is as clean a place as I've ever seen."

A murmur of agreement rose in the room.

"It *was* me—and please call me Michael. I believe it was this gentleman," he indicated Bill, "who asked me the question about the custodial staff. I'm afraid I didn't make myself heard above the crowd. It wasn't four to five thousand—"

Don thought, *Okay, then. I knew it wasn't that many.*

"The number was 45,000," Michael continued.

Carmen gasped, and gave a quick laugh. Don looked thunderstruck. Alan voiced what Carmen and the others had suddenly realized. "So everyone's part of the custodial crew?"

"Yes, exactly. The cleanliness of the park is crucial. It's part of what makes the Magic Kingdom truly magic. It's so important to us that we all consider ourselves part of the custodial crew."

Bill wondered how this was built into the policies and procedures. Cleanliness was clearly an automatic, even instinctive, value in the park, but what made it work? The bank had established customer service policies, but adherence to most of them seemed to fall by the wayside.

"Is there a policy for this?" he asked. "And if so, how do you make it stick?"

"No real policy," came the reply, "but park cleanliness is part of the culture here. And I think one of the reasons is the leadership displayed by cast members at all levels."

Oh, no, Don thought. *Now we're going to get into all that leadership mumbo-jumbo.* "What exactly does that mean?" he asked aloud.

Mort stood and faced the group, speaking loud enough for the entire room to hear. "Perhaps I can help out here. Yesterday we saw Michael pick up a piece of paper and toss it into a trash can. Every time that happens—which is anytime Michael sees trash in the park—that says more about the importance of cleanliness than any policy or procedure that could ever be written."

"I appreciate that, Mort," said Michael. "But just as important, probably more so, is the fact that every supervisor does the same thing. Dick Nunis, chairman of Walt Disney Attractions, and Judson Green, president of Walt Disney Attractions, pick up litter along with everybody else. So this commitment to cleanliness is ingrained in everyone's mindset.

"The commitment goes all the way back to Walt Disney himself. He used to take his daughter to carnivals, and he just couldn't believe how dirty the places were. He envisioned something without the carny atmosphere—the kind of place a parent wouldn't hesitate to take a child."

His face grew serious. "We want to make sure that same mindset is instilled in every new cast member. So during Traditions, which is the first training session everyone attends, our new cast members are shown two pictures: a street outside the park and Main Street, here in the park. Compared to the park, the outside street is chaos. The buildings are all different styles and ages, some in need of repair. There's paper and trash in the street. Nothing fits together. Main Street is always impeccably clean and all the buildings and accoutrements are true to the period. People look at one picture ... then the other ... then everyone begins to understand the importance of keeping the park clean."

"So, how do you keep it going?" Bill asked, back to his original question.

"At this point, it's one of those things that just happens," said Michael. "Nobody talks about it, but nobody thinks of doing it any other way. I was talking with one cast member about a week ago. She'd been here about a month. I asked her what impressed her most vividly about the Magic Kingdom.

"She said that when her manager showed her around to introduce her to her station—she works on Main Street—they'd be talking, and every time he saw a piece of trash, which wasn't very often, he'd bend over and pick it up. It's little things like that that set the tone and help commit *everyone* to walking the talk.

"One of the advantages we have now is that we can transport that commitment. When we opened Wilderness Lodge, for example, 80 percent of the cast members there had already worked elsewhere in Walt Disney World. Does that answer your question?" Michael asked Bill.

"Yes, but I've got one more. Why do you use 'Traditions' as your term for new-employee orientation?"

"We don't have employees," Michael reminded the group, "we have cast members. That's an important distinction in our culture. So we don't think of ourselves as 'orienting' cast members—instead, we're passing down traditions. If you're a new cast member at Disney World, you go through Traditions. Everyone goes—"

He paused and with a sweeping gesture took in the whole room.

"Including me. Although I attended Traditions at Disneyland, it was in a room almost exactly like this one."

Hearing this, Bill thought about the customer service programs at his bank. He had never attended one—they were for people in "customer service positions." He doubted that the bank president had attended any either, yet she always emphasized that creating and keeping customers was what the bank was all about. *If the customers were so important,* he thought now, *why didn't everybody attend those programs?* Clearly what was needed at his bank was more "walking the talk."

"But, Michael," said Carmen, "if everyone's part of everything—the custodial crew, Traditions, and everything else—don't the lines of authority sometimes get blurred? Do you ever find yourself wondering who's in charge?"

Michael smiled. "Well, the *guest* is always in charge. But, yes, sometimes lines of authority can get blurred. The other morning, I was walking though the park with several executives from the company. One of the cast members came up to me and pointed out that I didn't have my name tag on—and that everyone is supposed to wear a name tag. I heard about that for the rest of the day.

"But at the same time, when each person feels in charge, even in a temporary or local way, that person takes her responsibility seriously. She 'owns' her job or a piece of the park or a situation. And that makes her care about it and take the guest's welfare personally. That's exactly how we cast members feel. So when I was reminded about my own name tag, I appreciated that cast member's concern about upholding our traditions, thanked him, and immediately found a name tag and put it on."

Michael went on. "That's one of the lessons Mort's been teaching your group, I believe—'walking the talk.' And you've probably been hearing about attention to detail, too. Right? Well, what that cast member did illustrates both points. He was paying attention to details—the universal wearing of name tags—and upholding the tradition that everyone walks the talk. They're different things, but connected. Each supports the other. None of our traditions stands alone."

Mort stood up and said, "I can give many other examples. Dick Nunis often does what we call a good show–bad show walk-through, looking for just one kind of detail—chipped paint, for example. Whenever he does that, he's walking the talk about attention to detail."

"How do you teach people to walk the talk or pay such amazing attention to detail?" asked Carmen.

"These things aren't so much taught, in the formal sense of the word, as they are learned by the cast in a variety of ways," answered Mort.

"I'm not sure I understand the difference."

Mort explained, "Whenever Dick Nunis looks for chipped paint, cast members—including Dick Nunis and Michael Eisner—learn, or are reminded, that attention to detail is important. It's much more likely to be learned this way than if there were a written policy or a notice on the bulletin board that said, 'Attention to detail is important.'"

Michael chimed in. "Ralph Waldo Emerson made the same point much more eloquently than either Mort or I could. He said, 'What you do thunders above your head so loudly, I cannot hear the words you speak.'"

"It sounds as if this approach makes a real difference in the way people deal with their work," Carmen commented. "Does it stick? How long does walking the talk last?"

"A lot longer than you might guess," Michael said. "But there's someone else in the room who can give you a better answer than I can." He looked up and motioned to someone in the back of the room. "Marvin, would you come up here and tell us your story?"

> **" *Emerson said it so eloquently: 'What you do thunders above your head so loudly, I cannot hear the words you speak.'* "**

Marvin, a tall, slim, black-haired man of about thirty-five, got to his feet. He got almost as much applause as Michael had received, as well as a shout from a young man on the far side of the room, "Yo! Dude!" Marvin was obviously well known and well liked.

"Well, it's kind of interesting," Marvin began quietly, as though unaccustomed to speaking in front of groups. "I left Disney World in 1993 because I had an opportunity to make more money working at a resort in northern Florida.

"I'd been there for nearly three years and had no intention of leaving. Then one weekend I was serving as duty manager and got a call at the front desk from a guest about a problem with his condo. The couple had been complaining for several days, in fact, and no one had solved their problem, or even really talked to them about it. So what I had was two guests who were madder than hornets."

In the audience, Judy was nodding vigorously. Upset customers was something she knew about.

"I went over to their place and sat down with them to talk things over," Marvin continued, acknowledging Judy with a smile. "After about twenty minutes, the gentleman stopped me and said, 'You're not from here, are you?'

" 'No, not originally,' I told him. 'But I've been working here almost three years.'

"Then he asked me, 'Were you ever with the Disney organization?'

" 'Sure,' I told him, 'I worked there for thirteen years.'

" 'Well,' he said, 'it shows. I could tell that you were willing to help us. That you were sympathetic to our situation. My wife and I worked at Disneyland when we were in college, and we remember how good it felt to be part of that team, to go out of our way to be helpful.'

"It's funny," said Marvin. "I thought to myself, *Why am I working here when I could be working for number one?* So I came back."

A murmur of appreciation and a scattering of applause filled the room. Marvin raised a finger and the audience grew quiet again.

"I think that's true of most cast members. Certain things get ingrained in you. That's just the way you do things. I was a big fan, I am a big fan, and even if I were to end up going somewhere else again, I'll still be a big fan. I've got Pixie Dust," he confessed.

"I keep hearing this 'Pixie Dust,' " said Judy. "Can you tell me what it is?"

"It's a special feeling about this place," Marvin told her. "People wash dishes and serve meals just like they do in lots of other restaurants, they work in stores and sweep streets just like they do in cities all around the world. But the commitment is different.

"And that commitment to quality stays with you wherever you go. You can take the Marvin out of Disney, but you can't take the Disney out of Marvin." This earned Marvin more applause and a couple of piercing whistles as he sat down.

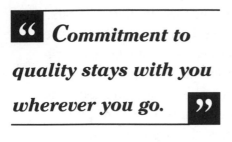

" *Commitment to quality stays with you wherever you go.* **"**

Later, at a sidewalk cafe, Mort, Don, Bill, Alan, and Judy sat at a table. There was one empty chair, which they held for Carmen.

"That is one motivated group!" explained Judy. "This organization really has a way of energizing people, doesn't it?"

"If you'd asked me about walking the talk yesterday," said Alan, "I would have said sure, absolutely, do it all the time. Today, I'm not so sure. I think Disney has raised the bar—Michael, Marvin, and a lot of other people we've met. I'll have to think about this for a while, but I'm beginning to get some ideas about changes we can make at my company."

"Well, here's one thing for you to think about," said Mort. "A lot of managers would be shocked to find out how little their employees believe management walks the talk. It's not that they're not giving it some effort. It's just that they're not giving it 100 percent effort— and 100 percent is critical."

Mort turned to Don. "Don, are you finding any of this useful?"

"Sure. Interesting," Don replied, but his tone of voice said, *Yeah, right.* Mort's eyebrows lifted slightly. He was beginning to consider Don a hard case.

"I've been thinking," said Bill, "about what would happen if someone walked up to the president of our bank and pointed out something like a missing name tag. Actually, I think she'd be fine with it, but I'm not so sure about the vice presidents—including me. And yet here, even Dick Nunis goes around looking for chipped paint." The admiration in Bill's voice was clear.

"The thing about all cast members attending Traditions really impressed me, too," he continued. "I knew everyone was called a cast member, but I thought that meant employees, not management. But Traditions made more sense when I realized 'everybody' means just that—everybody is a cast member! In other places, Traditions would be interpreted as 'Do as we say, not as we do.' Here, it's 'We're all in this together!' "

Just then, Carmen rejoined the group.

"You missed my speech," joked Bill.

"I was being aggressively friendly," said Carmen. "I saw a family taking pictures, so I offered to take their picture for them." She grinned at Mort. "Does that make me a cast member?"

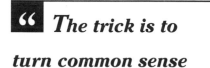

" *The trick is to turn common sense into common practice.* "

"Of course," laughed Mort. "I have application blanks for all of you. Anybody else ready to sign up?"

"Why, sure, Mort," said Judy. "That's the only reason I came here, don't you know?"

"Carmen, we were just talking over our session with Michael and Marvin," Alan said.

"Yes. Wasn't that interesting? It really gave me something to think about. As I listened to Michael talking, I began thinking that what he was saying was really common sense. But then I also realized that most companies don't really practice these common-sense things. The real key is turning common sense into common practice. I especially liked his answer to my question about the number on the custodial staff. In total, our company has 620 employees. Now, we couldn't get away with calling them cast members—wouldn't even want to. But I've been thinking about walking the talk, as you put it. If we could set that standard the way they do here, we could have 620 employees on the custodial staff, 620 on the sales team, 620 on the customer service staff—and on, and on. Everything would stay cleaner, run better, and attend to the customer's needs better."

The others smiled and nodded in agreement, obviously already thinking about ways to put some of these ideas to use at their own places of business. Don wasn't nodding, but he did look thoughtful.

"You're absolutely right," said Mort. "The point is not that Michael Eisner picks up paper. The point is that everyone walks the talk. And the most important thing at your company is that everyone walks the talk. Now, let's head over to the Hall of Presidents and see what we can learn there."

THE IMPORTANCE OF THINGS UNSEEN

Day 2, 1:35–2:45 P.M.

Having slipped backstage between shows, they stood face to face with the presidents. Washington, Jefferson, Lincoln, Teddy Roosevelt, all the Mount Rushmore faces and more. The Gang of Five was, as a group, not easily awed by authority or fooled by mannequins, but none—and from Don's expression, he seemed as impressed as the rest—could ignore the reverence they felt standing before these giants, all of whom were remarkably lifelike, and who moved, smiled, and spoke almost as though they were the real heroes, resurrected from history.

"Look, Bill," whispered Judy, when they came to the part of the display that included the modern presidents. "Clinton's wearing his Iron Man watch."

Bill smiled. "Shows the correct time, too," he said.

Carmen's interest was drawn to what the presidents were wearing. Vintage clothing was one of her passions, and she noticed quickly that the clothing styles appeared to be true to each period. Another example of attention to detail, obviously.

"Mort, their clothes look authentic," she said. "Are these actual period costumes, or are they replicas?"

"They're replicas. But they were made using materials that were available back then. You're very observant, Carmen. Are you a student of old clothing styles?"

As he spoke he remembered the brightly painted fabric of the T-shirt she'd worn yesterday. Today the unusual nubby fabric of her dress had drawn his notice too. She obviously paid a lot of attention to workmanship and style.

"Yes," Carmen said, "but I wouldn't have known these were reproductions. Except that most of the actual pieces I've seen in museums don't look this good. It's hard to preserve old clothes."

"There's something else about these garments you may have noticed," said Mort. "Look closely at the stitching, especially in Washington's and Jefferson's shirts."

"Yes, I saw that. Are they really hand-stitched?"

"Yes, they are. And I'll tell you something else. Not only are the fabrics woven using the old methods, but the stitches used to sew them together are exactly true to period."

Carmen smiled. "I thought they looked real, but even so, from this distance there's no way I could have told the difference. And from where they're sitting, I'll bet that not one guest in a million would even notice the sewing, much less be able to tell whether the stitching is authentic. I know attention to detail is important to Disney's culture, but couldn't this be considered overkill?"

Amen, thought Don.

"You might say that," replied Mort, "if this were simply an example of fanatical attention to detail—and I'm sure we can all agree it is rather fanatical.

"But that's not the point. It's true that guests are not going to see this level of detail. It won't factor into their experience here—at least, not directly. Guests will never know the difference.

"But cast members will. That's the important thing. And that's what's behind our next lesson."

He handed out the next card.

L E S S O N 4

Everything walks the talk.

"You see, not only does every*one* have to walk the talk—so does every*thing*. And even though ninety-nine-point-nine percent of guests probably will never have your opportunity to learn about the special stitching, and even though many cast members haven't even seen the stitching, all of our cast members know about it. Everything here walks the talk, and that's just one example."

The others looked at Mort, hoping he'd reveal even more of Disney's secrets. He didn't disappoint them.

"Another example is the paint on the carousel. Each part that is supposed to be colored gold has been painted with 23-karat gold-leaf paint. Not gold-colored paint, but 23-karat gold-leaf paint! I seriously doubt that the kids can tell the difference between gold-leaf and gold-colored paint. Neither can their parents. Neither can most cast members. I sure can't.

"But," he emphasized, "all cast members know it's 23-karat gold-leaf paint. And that's important to them. It's just one way of letting them know that when it comes to our guests we go all out in everything we do."

"Why does it have to be gold leaf?" asked Judy.

"The gold-leaf paint is a reminder for cast members. It reminds us that our guests are the most important thing. Sometimes cleaning up the carousel is not a pleasant task, and we need to be reminded why we do it—for the kids, for our guests. The gold-leaf paint is a very important symbol.

"You see, it would be easy to do the job halfway and excuse it by saying, 'What's the point of paying fanatical attention to detail on something that guests won't even notice?' "

Don scowled, thinking of the kid's gum yesterday. Mort went on, undaunted by Don's expression.

"The real gold reminds us that we take care of the equipment, the facilities, the grounds for all our guests, because guests are our true gold, our reason for existence. If it weren't for them, we wouldn't exist. No guests, no nothing."

"I like that philosophy," said Alan. "Of course, we all try to keep the customer foremost in mind, whatever our business. Sometimes we don't do everything we could, though. I'm going to remember your gold-leaf paint when I get back and see if I can figure out how to use that concept to—"

Judy interrupted. "Wait a minute, Alan. Tell them what you told me about the business cards."

"Oh, right," Alan said. "A few years ago, we began to realize that our employees had concluded—based either on previous experience or experience at our company—that only 'important people' got business cards. So we decided to give everyone a business card.

"Then we had to figure out what to put on the cards. At first we were going to use just the individual's name and job title—Sales Manager, Administrative Assistant, Accountant, whatever. But then one of the people who write code said that, since the company president liked to talk about the importance of our customers, why didn't we put 'Manager of Customer Relations' on everyone's card?"

The thought of entertaining the opinions of what amounted to a software company's version of a production worker at a *managers'* meeting was too much for Don—not to mention the idea of issuing every employee a business card. "If everybody's card says the same thing," he argued, "what's the point of having them? And what does that cost you, anyway?"

"Well, I think it's a super idea!" said Judy.

Alan said to Don, "Some of our own people thought it was silly to have cards, too. Others thought it was great, and the rest basically shrugged. Eventually, what we put on everyone's card was two things: the person's original job title and 'Customer Relations Associate.'

"But the truth of the matter is that this small, inexpensive action—and it *was* inexpensive, Don—has brought about a huge change in the way our people look at their jobs. That business card is a constant reminder that everyone needs to focus on providing what customers want—even people who never come in direct contact with a customer.

"In fact, we think the customer is so important that when I meet with each new employee the first week to explain how important the customer is, something I've been doing since we started, I now give each one a set of business cards to build that customer focus from day one."

"What does your card say, Alan?" Bill asked.

Alan took out one of his business cards and handed it to Bill, who read it out loud: " 'Alan E. Zimmerman, President and Customer Relations Associate.' "

"That's great," said Bill, returning it. "That's really walking the talk!"

"I agree," said Mort. "And, Alan, the more things like that that you can build into your operating environment, the more every employee will feel included and the stronger the culture will be."

> **" *Everyone needs to focus on providing what customers want—even people who never come in direct contact with customers.* "**

"Well, then, Mort," said Judy, "how about things that don't walk the talk? Wouldn't they tend to weaken the culture? How do you keep that from happening?"

Mort smiled back. "Good question, Judy. The design people here have a word for something that doesn't walk the talk: they call it an 'intrusion.' When they come up with a theme and begin to lay out the design, they look for potential intrusions—things that don't belong.

"Some are fairly obvious. As we walk around, look at the food carts in each land. They're all designed to match the theme of their area. They don't get moved from one area to another. The Liberty Square popcorn wagon is themed to match the Liberty Square area and nowhere else.

"Ever notice that you never see a cast member dressed in Frontierland clothes walking through Fantasyland?" As the Gang of Five nodded in agreement, Mort smiled and waved for them to follow as he opened a door and started down a flight of stairs.

Thirty minutes later they emerged from a vast subterranean level. The Disney World the guest sees, they had discovered, is really the "second story." Underneath is a massive tunnel that not only allows cast members to get from the locker rooms to their locations without being seen, but also provides a way to distribute food and merchandise and have access to all the utilities. They had seen the main wardrobe room, a cafeteria, break rooms, a barber shop, and stairs up to the various Magic Kingdom areas. Even Don was impressed.

"Now that's pretty massive," said Mort. "Other things are less massive but equally important—like trash cans. You'll see right away that many trash cans are custom painted and custom decorated to fit a particular area. But sometimes the designers go beyond just paint and decoration.

"For example, because it's a campground Fort Wilderness generates more direct trash and refuse from guests than, say, a hotel property. Now, no one wants bags of trash sitting out by the curb, so the designers created trash cans that were molded in fiberglass, then painted and aged to look like tree stumps. The fiberglass didn't hold up when it was half buried, so they switched to concrete.

"I don't know exactly what all this cost, but someone once told me Disney has some very expensive trash cans. The important thing, though, is that the trash cans are just one way that everything walks the talk.

"Another example would be Typhoon Lagoon. The story line underlying this concept is that a typhoon hit a certain area with such strong winds that everything was washed inland to where it now sits. So there's a tugboat sitting on top of a mountain with water spouting out of the smokestack every hour on the hour, and it has whistles that chime the time as well.

"All of these elements combine to walk the talk. The tugboat was washed to the top of this mountain, which shows how strong the winds were, and the spouting water shows that the typhoon didn't happen too long ago. There's a tremendous amount of time, energy, and money spent to come up with a concept that's different from what's been done anywhere else in the world. If everything didn't support that, much of it would have been wasted.

"John Hench, the guy I mentioned who did the colors, told me a story that I think helps put everything in perspective. When the designers were putting together Liberty Tree Tavern, Walt told him there was one basic concept: 'I want people to go into a five-million-dollar building and buy a five-cent hamburger.' The price of hamburgers has gone up since Walt's day, but the premise of giving them great value is still there. You can't get too fanatical with a hamburger—after all, a hamburger is just a hamburger—but you can give them a fantastic place to enjoy the hamburger.

"Using the word 'Traditions' rather than 'orientation' is another way everything walks the talk. In fact, it goes even deeper than that; everything about Traditions walks the talk. Participants in Traditions sit at round tables. We use round tables for a purpose: to foster the concept of teams. New cast members learn about teamwork by working in teams, not just by listening to someone talk about teamwork."

"Let me see if I understand," said Bill. "By 'attention to detail,' you mean details that directly affect the visitors' experience here; but when you say, 'Everything walks the talk,' you're talking about something that more indirectly affects the experience."

"That's right," Mort said. "Think of 'everything walks the talk' in terms of being aligned or congruent with your purpose. If you're going to talk about teamwork, why not have people *work* in teams? When people really begin walking the talk, it's easy to realize that *things* need to walk the talk too. So 'everyone' means Eisner, Nunis, ticket takers, equipment operators, everyone in the cast. 'Everything' means the tables in the training room, the employee newsletter, the hiring process—all are congruent with the Disney philosophy and character.

"And, sure, everything walking the talk does affect the guest's experience, but in ways he or she is frequently not aware of. And that's the way it should be. Things that walk the talk should by and large be invisible to guests.

"For instance, some of you probably know Disney World has its own energy system and its own fire department. Those are support systems; they make sure the Magic Kingdom runs smoothly. Many large organizations have the same thing. The 'walk the talk' piece of Disney's fire department is that the building is painted to the theme of *101 Dalmatians.* The next time you're over there, check out the side of the building. You can't miss it—it's white with black spots. Many cast members pass it on the way to and from work every day. It's a constant reminder of what the Magic Kingdom is all about.

"And the newsletter for cast members—it's called *Eyes and Ears.* That's not surprising. In fact, it would be surprising to have it called anything else. Most companies do something similar with their employee newsletters—the name usually says something about what the company does. The difference I've observed is that in most companies it's a case of a few things walking the talk. Here, and in other world-class companies, it's a case of *everything* walking the talk.

"Here's one last example. When guests arrive in the morning, they hear lively music; cast members are upbeat and energetic when they greet guests. But in the evening, the music's mellow; cast members act more relaxed.

"That difference is planned and deliberate. It's done that way to stay in tune with the guests' moods.

"Every guest comes in through the main gate and leaves through the main gate. So every guest who stays through most of the day experiences this. The music enhances the experience; it adds to the guest's feeling of satisfaction and well-being; it makes the guest remember the visit pleasurably and want to return. But not one in a thousand will be aware of this musical difference.

"Would it matter if guests noticed? Probably not. They'd probably appreciate it. After all, who wants to walk into the Magic Kingdom all excited, only to be greeted by a mellow, laid-back cast member? And who wants to finish a long day in the Magic Kingdom, heading for the main gate, tired but happy, and have to put up with excited cast members hopping up and down?"

Judy laughed, a little nervously. The idea gave her pause. She tended to be a cheerleader, always on, always up and excited. Maybe it wasn't necessary. Maybe, once in a while, people would like her to be a little more mellow. Especially when it was hard to stay upbeat, when she had to force herself. She'd have to check out the greeters in the evening and see.

Carmen thought about how she often deliberately chose her outfit to create a particular impression with her staff or customers. Now, she wondered, how could she apply the everything-walks-the talk idea in more significant ways in her business?

Even Don looked thoughtful, as though considering that this idea might, after all, work in his own firm.

PUTTING ON THE EARS

Day 2, 3:00–3:30 P.M.

They were walking past the entrance to Frontierland. A few steps ahead of Mort, Carmen was reflecting on what she was learning, impressed by how completely the design and execution of every action and every detail at Disney was carried out with a careful eye to its ultimate effect on the visitor—and that had made her wonder. How did they know how they were doing? How did they measure customer satisfaction?

She stopped walking to let Mort catch up. Then she said, "Look, I know every business has to focus on customer satisfaction, sure, but few businesses are as directly connected to so many customers as this one. The business of Disney World seems to take place mostly between individual cast members and individual guests. So I must assume the cast members have a way of getting feedback from your visitors on whether or not you've succeeded.

"But if your guests are like everyone else today, they're probably over-surveyed. We've got a customer satisfaction survey—I assume most companies do. How about Disney? How do they go about analyzing their overall success? How do they find out what individual guests like and don't like about their experience, and how does that affect plans and policies?"

"There are lots and lots of things involved in that process, Carmen," Mort answered. "And the reason I say that has to do with our next lesson."

Don, walking close enough to overhear this conversation, found his interest piqued. He moved closer to Mort, thinking that he might glean some useful information from this. Through all the hocus-pocus woo-woo stuff he had been hearing about attention to detail and walking the talk, he remembered reading about Disney's research methods.

"Mort," he asked, "I've heard that you use laptop computers on site to survey guests. Is that true?" In Don's mind, the use of computers was at least a tiny indication that something serious was going on, something grounded in data and technology.

"We do," Mort answered. "We find computers very helpful in recording guests' impressions in real time— that is, while everything is fresh in their minds. The cast members who do this are called Super Greeters. Their principal role is to walk around all day and make sure the guests are happy. They wear special shirts identifying them as Walt Disney World Super Greeters.

"Each Super Greeter carries a pager and responds immediately to a call. If an attraction has to go off-line for some reason, cast members there page the Super Greeters, who go immediately to that attraction to assist guests who have been inconvenienced. That's a major portion of their job.

"But another of their important job responsibilities is to survey guests. They carry laptop computers and key in each response immediately. The Super Greeters collectively survey 700 to 1,400 guests a week. The results are aggregated and fed back to the cast each week. This feedback is very important. It tells us how close we're getting to 100 percent guest satisfaction."

"Aren't you in danger of boring your guests?" asked Carmen. "I know that some of the surveys I get are pretty boring. Most of them, in fact."

"Well, think about that for a minute," said Mort. "If you were a Disney cast member, how would you approach that problem? Remember the points we've covered."

"Well . . ." Carmen pursed her lips for a moment, thinking. Then she said, "I guess I'd pay close attention to detail—and remember that everything walks the talk. So, with that in mind. . . ." She paused. "I'd look for a way to make the survey part of the overall experience. I'd try to make it entertaining."

"Sure!" said Judy. "You could have Tinkerbell do the survey! Oh, but you already said the Super Greeters do it, didn't you?"

"Actually, you're right on both counts," said Mort, smiling. "The Super Greeter does the actual inputting of the information, but in a very real way Tinkerbell conducts the survey. The computer program uses Tinkerbell and other Disney characters to liven up the process. They're built right in. We've found that guests really enjoy being surveyed."

Alan was already thinking about how he could incorporate that into his company. His company wasn't Disney—fun wasn't their thing—but that didn't mean they couldn't build some entertainment value into their survey techniques. Many of his employees had a lively sense of humor—not surprising in a group of intense, creative, super-smart programmers. Surely that creativity could be put to use revising the company's survey forms.

"As you can see," continued Mort, "the way the survey is conducted is an example of everything walking the talk. It's not so much a detail that's there to enhance the guest's experience as it is the integration of a Disney theme into every aspect of the experience. The guest knows she's being interviewed as though Tinkerbell were asking the questions, but, in effect, it's merely background to the guest who is focusing on providing answers to our questions.

"But the survey itself is an example of the fifth lesson." With that, Mort handed everyone a card with these words:

LESSON 5

Customers are best heard through many ears.

He waited as they all read the cards. When they looked up at him again, he continued.

"What this means," he said, "is that having the Super Greeters survey guests is only one of the ways we look at how we're doing. It's a very important way, but it's not the only way. If it were, we'd be listening to only one source, and through only one vehicle. We think it's crucial to survey guests, but it's equally important to use other tools and tap other sources of information about how we're doing. Some tools are formal, such as the laptop survey—" and here he looked over at Don. "And some are very informal.

"Here's one example. A restaurant may have twenty-five cast members waiting tables on several shifts. It's hard to get all twenty-five together at once to talk about improving things. Instead, all cast members on a single shift spend a few minutes evaluating how the day went, on a scale of one to ten.

"Maybe it's a seven. So why is it a seven? What needs to change to make it a ten? They keep track of problems and take action to solve them. At the next meeting, each problem is brought up again to see if improvements are happening and how the guests are reacting.

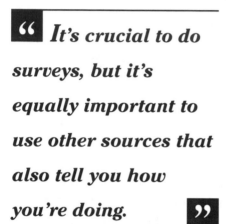

" It's crucial to do surveys, but it's equally important to use other sources that also tell you how you're doing. "

"Now, these discussions may be part of a formal process, but more often than not, they're something that just happens. It's part of the culture. It's the way things are.

"Here's another example. Several years ago, upper management felt that the menu in the Disney restaurant needed changing—that the one they had was old and tired. Well, the waitstaff got together and decided that the management viewpoint was wrong. So they went to Dick Nunis and told him the menu was just fine.

"In fact, the guests who ate there *loved* the menu. It was only the executives who had grown tired of it. The waitstaff insisted that the menu should stay exactly the same, so it did."

"The same thing happened in my company," said Alan. "We had some marketing materials we'd been using for fourteen months that I thought we should change. I was tired of them. Even sales and marketing thought it would be fun to develop some new ones. But the truth of the matter was that both our field sales reps and our customers loved the stuff. It worked."

Judy said, "All the same, I can think of several instances where either I or someone else at the company held onto things for too long. How do you know when to change and when not to?"

Carmen answered her: "I think the real issue is whether or not the thing in question is delivering value in some form to the customer."

"Good point," said Mort. "For example, when Epcot first opened, you never saw Mickey, Goofy, or Minnie there. We believed guests would think they were out of place there. In fact, it was just the opposite. Guests complained about not seeing them. So we changed the visitation schedule, and now some characters also visit Epcot."

"Sounds like some of your multiple listening posts are just cast members listening directly to individual guests," said Bill.

"At the core, all our listening posts are about cast members listening to guests—as opposed to listening to each other or themselves. The executives who wanted the menu changed were listening to themselves; the waitstaff was listening to the guests.

"**A**nd here's one of our best listening posts coming this way now. Nicole, would you come over here and help me teach my lesson?"

A smiling woman joined the group. Mort introduced her to the Gang of Five. "Nicole has been here for fourteen years," he said. "Nicole, we were just talking about the different ways Disney listens to its guests. Could you give them an example from your own experience?"

"Sure," she replied. "Let's see . . . how about this one? Several years ago I was food and beverage manager at the Polynesian Hotel. It was the Fourth of July, a very busy night. In fact, it was so busy that we took over a banquet room normally used for conventions and turned it into a restaurant for the evening, and even then people had to wait up to an hour for a table.

"I happened to be standing in the lobby when a man came up to ask the hostess how much longer until his table was ready. She told him thirty minutes. He went back to where his wife was standing. I was going the same direction. As I passed, I overheard him apologizing to her. Apparently, it was their tenth anniversary and he had forgotten to make reservations.

"At this point I had two choices. I could keep on walking or I could do something about the situation. So I went back to the hostess and suggested that she give them the next available table—and that we tell their waiter that it was their tenth anniversary. That's what she did, and we ended up brightening their visit."

"Oh, sure," said Don. "But weren't the people in line ahead of the couple angry when they saw them being seated first?"

"Not really," Nicole said. "As soon as the couple was gone, the hostess told the rest of the people why they had seated them ahead of everyone else. They were happy to be part of the whole thing. Remember, I told you how the cast members' positive attitude often rubs off on the guests."

"Pixie Dust," Judy said.

"Pixie Dust," Mort laughed.

"Is this unusual?" Bill asked. "Or does this sort of thing go on all the time?"

"It happens a lot," Nicole continued. "One cast member, a custodial host, volunteered to take a picture of a couple. They said, 'Oh, this will be great, because we're on our honeymoon!' They told him they were on their way to the Chefs de France Cafe at Epcot to have dinner. So he went to his supervisor and told her what a nice couple they were and that they were here on their honeymoon and that he'd like to do something special for them.

❝ *Listening posts are about the company listening to customers—as opposed to listening to itself.* ❞

"The supervisor said, 'Sure, whatever you think is appropriate.' Well, we just happen to have a flower shop over in 'France' that has fresh-cut flowers. So the cast member went there, got a big bunch of flowers, and delivered it to them at the restaurant, courtesy of the entire cast of Disney World.

"Now, if the custodial host had not been so helpful—it's that thing we call being 'aggressively friendly' that Mort probably already has described to you—he wouldn't have had the opportunity to talk to them. And had he not had the opportunity to talk to them, he wouldn't have been able to function as a listening post.

"It happens in a lot of different ways, too. Someone in housekeeping hears about a birthday and notifies the restaurant; a waitperson hears about an anniversary and arranges for a fancy dessert. Cast members know that they can *each* do something that makes that visit special.

"Think of it this way," said Nicole. "We have some 45,000 cast members. That gives us 90,000 ears. Think of that collection of ears as one giant listening post all by itself, without even counting all the other ways we can— and do—listen to guests."

"So there are actually two ways cast members act as listening posts," said Alan. "Formal listening, like surveys to collect data about guest satisfaction, and informal listening that takes care of something at that point in time."

"Oh, there are lots more ways than just those two," said Nicole. "Some are really simple, but very powerful in improving guest satisfaction. Let's say, for example, that someone walks up to a popcorn stand and asks the cast member for a guide map, and there aren't any. No one's thought of stocking them. The cast member makes a note of the request. Every time it happens again, the cast member marks a tally. If it happens more than a few times, guide maps will probably be made available at or near that popcorn stand, because there's evidence that guests need maps in that particular area.

"Sometimes the best tools are the simplest. I mean, we use focus groups and other marketing tools like everyone else, but if we overlooked information from cast members, we'd be overlooking probably the most valuable source of information we have—people who have hundreds of thousands of contacts with our guests every day. And guests are what Disney is all about.

"You think that about covers it, Mort?"

"Thanks, Nicole," said Mort. "You've been a big help. Now they know I'm not just making this stuff up."

Carmen thought about what Nicole had just told them. Her company conducted customer satisfaction surveys, focus groups, and one-on-one discussions with customers, but no one in the company had the Disney cast member's ability to take action. The idea of tick marks was intriguing; her company had a system to tell them when a customer asked for something that was temporarily out of stock—but nothing to indicate when customers asked for something they didn't carry. Carmen took out her note pad and scribbled a reminder.

She heard Mort and Bill laugh. When she looked up, Judy was grinning and holding a set of big, black, round ears over her head. "How do you like my new hat?" she asked.

"When did you get those?" asked Bill.

"I've had them in my purse since I got here. You can probably tell, my daughter cut her teeth on them. I got 'em in the mail a few weeks after my second visit. See? There's a set of survey questions on the back. I decided to keep the ears, so I made a copy to fill out and sent that in instead.

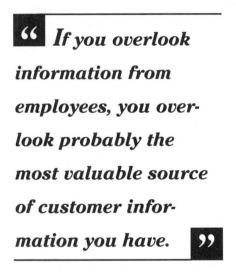

❝ *If you overlook information from employees, you overlook probably the most valuable source of customer information you have.* ❞

"Anyway, isn't this just about the coolest survey form you ever saw? And it's a good example of multiple listening posts, too."

Alan had a sudden insight. His company had just introduced a new bundle of utility software programs and was following up each purchase with a questionnaire. But survey returns were low, making the data next to useless. *What would happen,* he wondered, *if they included the ques-*

tionnaire in one of the printer utilities—as a test page, perhaps? Or maybe a survey form could be printed up to look like a floppy disk. Would either of those ideas improve the returns? He wrote a note to himself to check into those possibilities.

"As long as you're taking notes," said Mort, "let me summarize the benefits of multiple listening posts.

"Some listening posts allow you to take immediate action on information—surprise birthday cakes arranged by housekeeping, a special meal, flowers for a honeymoon couple. A cast member hears something and acts on it. If it involves a problem, if we didn't measure up to a guest's expectations, then we try to get to the root cause of the problem and make sure it doesn't happen again.

"Other kinds of listening posts track guests' needs and satisfaction levels—cast members' notes and tallies, after-visit surveys like Judy received, and the Super Greeters with laptops are good examples. There are still others we haven't mentioned. Phone surveys are a more formal kind of listening post. You can find out things over the phone that you can't get in writing—tone of voice tells you a lot, and you can probe for more information.

"Another example involves cast members who are supervisors. One of their job responsibilities is walking around and meeting guests. While they're chatting, they're also asking questions to see how things are going—taking the temperature, so to speak.

"No single source could give us everything we need. Each listening post gives us a slightly different view of things. It's like the seven blind men and the elephant— to one an elephant is like a rope, to another a tree. With multiple listening posts, we get a balanced view of the different ways our guests experience Disney World, and we get specifics from particular points of view."

Carmen was wondering how Disney World handled letters from guests, satisfied or otherwise. "I came here with my family a few years ago," she told the group, "and a cast member went out of her way to help us. I wrote a letter to Disney World describing what she had done. Would that letter be an example of a listening post, Mort?"

"Without a doubt. Letters provide a window into how cast members please guests. In that sense, your letter was part of a listening post. It was the observation of one guest about one incident involving one cast member.

"Does the fact that it's one guest, one incident, and one cast member mean it's unimportant? On the contrary. Every guest is important, and letters like yours demonstrate the importance of every interaction with a guest."

KEEPING THE
MAGIC GOING

Day 2, 3:30–4:30 P.M.

"**Y**our letter most certainly went to a department called Guest Letters," Mort continued. "Then it went to the cast member's supervisor, who probably shared it with the cast member, and with other cast members. So it was not only a nice pat on the back for your helper, it also set a good example for all the others—this is how to wow a guest!

"The fact that your letter was read and shared among cast members and supervisors is an example of how to use a listening post effectively, of course. But the way your letter of praise was treated and used is also a demonstration of our sixth lesson."

He handed everyone a card.

L E S S O N   6

*R*eward, recognize, and celebrate.

"When letters like yours come in, it's a great opportunity to recognize and celebrate. I think I can show you better than tell you. The cast member—Carmen, do you remember her name?"

"I'll never forget it. Her name was Murphy," said Carmen.

"Okay," Mort went on. "Ever feel the urge to become an actor? No? Never mind, you'll look great compared to me. Let's try a little role playing. It'll give you an idea of how the situation would have unfolded." Carmen smiled and walked up next to Mort. "You and I will play the same character," Mort said. "Murphy's supervisor. All you have to do is repeat what you said in your letter. Okay?"

Carmen grinned. "I can't remember the *exact* words, but I can come pretty close."

"Great," said Mort. "Alan, would you stand by with the Oscar, please? Judy, get ready with the applause sign. Now, first, here's the supervisor in front of a group of cast members. He says, 'Here's a letter from a family who came all the way from New York. Murphy turned a minor difficulty into some real magic for them, and the mother wrote us a letter that I'd like to share with you.'"

With that, Mort held up an imaginary letter and nodded to Carmen, who said:

Dear Disney:

The four members of our family recently spent a delightful vacation at the Magic Kingdom. But one event made our visit seem truly magical.

We got to the front of the line at Space Mountain, only to find out that our little Gloria couldn't take her ice cream cone on the ride. Now, we should have realized this up front, but we were so excited to be there that we just weren't thinking.

Gloria broke into tears and we were all in a quandary about what to do. Then one of the staff members— Murphy—came over, bent down, and told Gloria that she would hold her ice cream for her and give it to her when she finished the ride. Gloria said, "Promise?" Then she gave Murphy her ice cream, and she thoroughly enjoyed the ride.

Sure enough, as we walked out the exit, there was Gloria's new friend with "her" ice cream cone. Now you and I both know what happened, because we know that an ice cream cone won't last twenty minutes on a summer afternoon in Florida. Murphy knew what time we would exit; she went to the nearest stand and bought a brand-new ice cream cone thirty seconds before we walked out the exit. Gloria said, "Thank you," but I'm sure she thought it was the same ice cream cone.

We know that someone went out of her way to make our visit special. Thanks so much for going above and beyond!

Your fan,

Carmen Rivera

Still in the role of supervisor, Mort lowered "his copy" of the invisible letter and addressed the group as though they were cast members:

" 'This is a great example of exceptional guest service. Murphy not only noticed the problem but came up with a creative solution. People like Carmen save their money to come here with their families, and each of us plays an important role in making it a magical experience for them. A special thanks to Murphy.' "

Then Mort once again became Mort. "Next, the supervisor would post the letter on the bulletin board so cast members could see exactly how one of their colleagues had affected someone's vacation in a positive way."

"Would that be considered reward, recognition, or celebration?" asked Bill.

"In this case, it's a combination of recognition and celebration," said Mort. "Mostly recognition. Recognition is about appreciating and acknowledging that someone has done something special. Certainly Murphy did something special in this situation, so she deserved recognition.

"The desire to be appreciated is one of the deepest of human yearnings. So Murphy had some of that need met by the letter. The additional recognition in front of other cast members also acknowledged Murphy's role as a valuable member of the team. A lot of organizations go through the motions of recognizing people, but only a few make it part of a *system*—the only way to make sure it happens."

Carmen was trying to put this all in perspective for herself. "My company has a lot of awards for the sales department—President's Club, Director's Club, that sort of thing. But there's really nothing for people who aren't in sales. The more I think about that, the more I think we should do something for the others, too."

"You might be right," said Mort. "Let me tell you about some other things that happen here, then we'll see what you think.

"One of the tools used is the Guest Service Fanatic card. It says, 'You have been recognized as a Guest Service Fanatic for (blank).' Managers walk around with these cards, hand them out to cast members, and thank them for their good deeds. The cast members drop their cards into a box. At the end of the month there's a drawing, and five or six cast members whose good deeds have given them a shot at it—the more good deeds, the better their chances—win prizes. The drawing's a big deal; there's a ceremony, fireworks, dancers. Either the vice president of the park or Mickey draws the names out of the box."

"What are your criteria for handing out these cards?" asked Bill.

"It depends on the area of responsibility, the principle that's being upheld. There are several areas, but let's look at two that we've talked about—service and teamwork.

"First, service. There are five standards."

He held up a finger.

"One: Always make eye contact and smile."

Then two fingers. "Two: Exceed guest expectations and seek out guest contacts.

"Three: Always give outstanding quality service. Four: Greet and welcome each and every guest. Five: Maintain a personal standard of quality in your work."

He had five fingers in the air at this point. He lowered his hand and began again.

"Then there are four guidelines for teamwork.

"One: Go beyond the call of duty. Two: Demonstrate strong team initiative. Three: Communicate aggressively with guests and fellow cast members. Four: Preserve the magical guest experience."

"That seems like a pretty explicit list of guidelines," said Bill. "Can't something like 'Make eye contact and smile' lead to rote behavior?"

"In theory, yes," said Mort, "and we've probably all experienced this. But keep in mind several things. First of all, it's not a list of rules, it's a list of guidelines surrounding our service standards. It provides managers with a tool—and a prompt—for recognizing the behaviors that we know help make a magical experience.

"More important, these guidelines don't operate in a vacuum. Every supervisor in the park models these behaviors. Every cast member has been through Traditions. Every cast member knows about the gold leaf on the carousel.

"Another company could come here and copy these standards word for word—and fall flat on its face because it wouldn't have everything else in place."

Bill nodded. He thought about all the piecemeal attempts his bank had made to improve customer loyalty. The results never seemed to last. Perhaps it was because they had never tried building it into the system.

"I'm still not sure what we're talking about here," Carmen said. "Is this reward, recognition, or celebration?"

"Yes, yes, and yes!" said Mort, smiling. "Yes, it's reward because people can win TVs, *Pocahontas* gift sets, and the like. Yes, it's recognition because the cards identify cast members and appreciated behaviors. And, yes, it's a ceremony of celebration, complete with fireworks and dancers. These things are not mutually exclusive."

"It sounds really cool," said Judy.

"But do you think it's fair that management gets to give out all the recognition cards?" asked Bill.

"Of course not," said Mort. "But that's probably why there's another form of recognition that comes from fellow cast members. It's called the Spirit of Disney Award. Another cast member has to nominate you for the award. You get a silver name tag for that."

"Oh, I like that!" said Judy.

"I'll give you an example," said Mort. "One cast member I know saw a woman sitting on a bench alone in the rain and went to her. The woman said she had just twisted her ankle and couldn't walk. The cast member— her name was Dot—immediately found an umbrella for her, then rounded up a wheelchair so she could get her out of the rain. She called for a nurse, and afterward arranged for someone to take her back to her hotel room.

"Later that same day, another cast member, who saw all this happening, nominated Dot for a Spirit of Disney Award."

Alan thought of the kinds of recognition people got in his firm. Too often, it seemed, it was a reprimand— not the kind of recognition people sought. "Is the feedback here always positive?" he asked.

"Not always," said Mort. "After the parade, supervisors post parade notes on the bulletin board. If a cast member did well, smiling and dancing around and entertaining the guests, the note would say something like 'Great job, Tony. Way to shake it!' On the other hand, if a cast member does a really substandard job, that's noted too. If it's just an okay job, nothing is posted."

"Do they try to post more positive feedback than negative feedback?" Judy asked.

"They don't try to, it just works out that way. Most cast members do a lot more things right than they do wrong. Disney's just reflecting what is actually going on."

Mort fell silent for a moment. Then he continued, "I get the opportunity to look behind the scenes at lots of companies besides Disney—and as an outsider at all of them, I can get a very good sense of what's really going on. Most, but not all, companies spend more time pointing out mistakes than achievements, even though people do more things right than wrong. A feedback ratio of one positive to three negative doesn't do much for morale.

"On the other hand, a ratio of three positive to one negative helps keep motivation and teamwork high. That's one reason I think the Spirit of Disney Award works so well—it boosts teamwork and it helps keep the ratio up around three positives to one negative. If one cast member helps another, the second can nominate the first for a Spirit of Disney Award.

"Think about what happens in your organizations. Your accounting department does a hundred things right, then makes a mistake on the hundred-and-first. Which one do they hear about?"

"Obviously, they hear about the mistake," said Carmen. "But they don't hear anything the other hundred times."

"What happens then?"

"Nothing."

"And that's exactly my point," said Mort. "They get yelled at for doing something wrong but nothing happens when they do something right. Psychologists have a term for what happens when there's no feedback. It's called 'extinction.' Reinforcement is positive feedback; punishment is negative feedback; extinction is no feedback. Unfortunately, no feedback is the most common response to good performance.

"Most companies acknowledge the importance of positive feedback, but don't do as good a job of practicing it as they could. Maybe because they don't understand the full impact of the difference between the three kinds of feedback. Think of it this way. Suppose you got careless and backed your car over your neighbor's flower bed. The neighbor comes out and yells at you. What kind of feedback is that?"

"Negative," said Alan.

"Right. And you expect it, don't you?

"Okay, forget the flower bed. You didn't back over it, and it's fine. Suppose, instead, you learn that your neighbor is ill, and you mow his lawn for him without being asked. Later, the neighbor comes over with a big chocolate cake and thanks you for helping out. What's that?"

"Reinforcement!" said Alan, Carmen, and Judy in unison.

"Exactly. And we all love positive feedback. Now, suppose you mow your neighbor's lawn because he's sick, and nothing happens. A week later, you mow it again. Once more, nothing happens. You see your neighbor get into his car to go to work. He waves to you casually as he drives by.

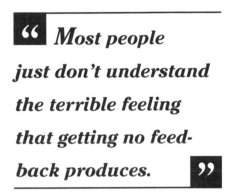

❝ *Most people just don't understand the terrible feeling that getting no feed- back produces.* ❞

"How does that make you feel?"

"Terrible!" said Alan.

"Extinct," said Bill. Judy and Mort laughed.

"You see my point, then," said Mort. "Most people understand positive feedback even though they don't practice it enough. And most people understand the negative impact of negative feedback. But most people just don't understand the terrible feeling that no feed- back leaves. Extinction—the absence of feedback—can cause people to withdraw their commitment.

"Getting no feedback can be just as devastating as getting negative feedback. Every time you see an employee or associate doing something that involves teamwork, walking the talk, paying attention to detail, listening to customers, or anything that helps delight your customers and keep them coming back—and you don't reinforce that behavior—there's a very high probability that person will feel just the way you would feel if your neighbor didn't thank you for your help.

"So I want you to keep that sense of what no feedback feels like in the front of your mind. And I want you to recognize each person for his or her contribution. It could be someone who works for you; it could someone in another department; it could be a supplier; it could even be a customer who helps you do a better job of delivering what he wants. It could be anyone at all who contributes to the goal, but the important thing is that you recognize that person's contribution.

"Not only is it the right thing to do, it helps customer satisfaction. People treat customers the same way they get treated. There are definite correlations between employee satisfaction and customer satisfaction."

Alan looked uncomfortable. "I have a confession to make," he said. "I think my positive-to-negative ratio is closer to one-to-three than three-to-one. I set the tone in my company, and I guess sometimes I'm a little bit hard on people who slip up or slack off, and often it doesn't even come to my attention when someone does something well."

"I guess I'm the same way, Alan," said Carmen. "Our relationship with the accounting department ranges between okay and awful. They do most things right for us. Then, one late report and we scald 'em. And it's not just my department, it's the whole company. It probably explains the strong silo effect that I've noticed, the way people seem concerned only with their own departments and not with the company as a whole. Obviously I need to rethink the way I'm dealing with my people, and try to get other departments to improve as well."

"That's what I need to do, too," said Alan. "But I'm not sure how to go about it. I'm afraid that one-to-three has become a habit for me now, and it's a hard habit to break." He looked at Mort.

" Extinction—the absence of feedback— can cause people to withdraw their commitment. "

"You're in luck," Mort told them. "I've got a simple, practical exercise that will help you. Remember, it's not as though you have to find three 'way-to-go's' every time you issue an 'aw shucks.' The idea is to average at least three positives to one negative over time—a week or a month, maybe.

"Here's what you do. At the beginning of the day, put ten dimes in your pocket or somewhere easily accessible.

"Every time you see someone doing something well—paying attention to detail, listening to customers, anything that helps wow your customers—I want you to recognize that person for her contribution.

"After you've done so, move a dime to another pocket. The next time you recognize someone, move another dime.

"Your goal is to get all ten dimes moved by the end of the day. Do it for thirty days and see how things have changed. I think you'll be pleasantly surprised."

"Why thirty days?" asked Bill.

"It takes most people twenty-one days to establish a new habit," said Mort. "I'm just adding a little insurance to make sure it really takes."

Judy finished jotting down some notes. "This is really helpful," she said. "If I'm hearing you right, you're saying to reinforce not just anything, but certain things—just the things that are going to help make our customers happy. I think I've been really good at giving positive feedback, but now that I think about it, I guess I'm giving it for anything and everything. Maybe I should be more careful and observant about what I'm reinforcing."

> **" *People treat customers the same way they get treated.* "**

"Exactly, that's really key," said Mort. "The important things are to make the feedback positive, make it immediate, and make it specific."

Don had been listening without comment, growing more and more restless and dissatisfied with this talk of positive and negative feedback. "I'm not at all sure I can agree with this," he said. "I pay people to do a good job.

Why should I give them special recognition for doing what I'm already paying them to do?"

"Well, let's see," said Mort. "What I hear you saying is that you pay people to take care in making products, so they should take care in making products."

"That's exactly what I'm saying!"

"Do you have people who *don't* take care in making products?" Mort asked.

"Of course!"

"Do they get paid?"

"Well, yes."

"So, in effect, you are paying them for not taking care in making products—because they aren't taking care, and you're paying them anyway."

Don frowned but did not reply. The point was well taken. He remembered how proud he'd been of his plant's record-setting numbers last quarter and how wounded he secretly felt when his boss didn't even mention their accomplishment.

Bill smiled. *Simple, but powerful,* he thought.

"Here's another way to think of reward and recognition. Put yourself in the shoes of the employee. She needs to make a living. That's the economic income— salaries, bonuses, fringe benefits, employee discounts, and so on. Then there's psychological income, which includes praise, letters of commendation, recognition ceremonies, celebrations, parties, and the like. People need both kinds of income."

"That's an interesting way of looking at it," said Carmen. "Which do you find is more important, economic or psychological income?"

"I think it would be better to let someone else answer that," Mort said. He began walking. "Let's go find a cast member to talk to."

A few minutes later they were in an offstage area with several cast members who were on a break. Mort greeted them and said, "I have some people here who are part of a study group to find out how you keep the Pixie Dust going in the Magic Kingdom. We were just talking about reward, recognition, and celebration. One of the questions was about which is more important, reward or recognition. What do you think?"

"What's the difference between them?" asked one of the cast members.

"Think of reward as meaning economic income and recognition as being psychological income," said Mort.

"Maybe I can answer that," said another cast member. "Hi, Mort. Remember me? I'm David. I helped you out last year when one of your group members needed a wheelchair." He extended his hand and Mort shook it.

"Yes, David, I certainly do. You go to the University of Massachusetts and work here in the summer, right?"

"That's right," said David, obviously pleased. "Well, it seems to me your question is like asking whether food or water is more important. The answer is that both are important. Without water, you'll die soon, probably in a few days. No food? You'll also die. It just takes longer.

"It's the same with pay and recognition. Pay is like water—gotta have it. But without some recognition, I'd just sort of wither on the vine. I'd be here physically, but my heart wouldn't.

"See that?" He pointed to a bulletin board covered with letters and photos. "Those are cards and letters from guests about how enjoyable we've made their vacations."

Another cast member, whose name tag read "Annie," said, "I got a letter once that's a perfect example of how important recognition is. It was from a little boy who was terminally ill. During his visit here, he collected a bunch of autographs. Then he lost the autograph book. I was handling the information line that day when his mom called. She was just devastated, and her only hope was that we might find the autograph book.

"I started calling around, trying to track it down. I called every place it might possibly be. I checked lost and found, the parking lot, everywhere. Nothing. So I called his mom and told her we couldn't find it. I also asked when they were leaving. There were two days left on their trip. I asked her whose autographs were in the book and what it looked like and everything. I told her to come to Guest Relations in two days and we'd have a book for her.

"So we got everything together. A new book with the autographs and everything. And two days later, the father came and picked it up. They were delighted to have the autographs, and I was delighted to be able to help them.

"I never got to see him. But about a month later, I got a thank-you card with a picture of the little boy. He died a week after he got the book. He'd enjoyed the autographs, though, and remembered the good time he'd had here. I still have the picture and the card. It was posted on the board for a while, but I keep it at home now. I'm still touched every time I look at it.

"I'm like David. I need to get paid. But it's things like that card that make me want to put my heart into every contact with every guest—especially on those days when I don't exactly get up on the right side of the bed."

After they left the cast members, they sat at a table near Main Street, uncharacteristically quiet.

Finally, Alan spoke. "Mort, I have to ask a question. Not everything Disney does is successful. For example, where does Disneyland Paris fit into this? We both know it was considerably less than a booming success."

"Well, there are a couple of things to keep in mind. First, a company that doesn't occasionally stub its toe is probably a company that's not trying anything new. The surest way to avoid mistakes is never to try new things. So one take on it is that Disney was trying something new.

"A second take is the reality of the situation. The average guest comes to Disney World for four nights and five days. The average guest goes to Disneyland Paris for one night and two days. Travel distances are shorter in Europe, and the economics work out differently.

"The third take is something I've observed about most successful organizations. The two most common by-products of phenomenal success are arrogance and complacency. To what degree did they possibly contribute to Disneyland Paris? I don't know.

> **❝ *The two most common by-products of phenomenal success are arrogance and complacency.* 🥂**

"Certainly no company or person is perfect. Everyone makes mistakes. Long-term success isn't about avoiding mistakes. It's about correcting those you do make as fast as possible."

"How about the theme park in Virginia that didn't go?" asked Alan.

"I personally thought it was a great idea," said Mort, "but Disney clearly picked the wrong location. They underestimated not only the number of people who might oppose it, but also their intensity and tenacity. Was it a mistake? Sure. But like I said, if you're trying new things, you're going to make some mistakes. That just comes with the territory.

"Any other questions?"

And when there were none, Mort wrapped up the day.

"I hope none of you were planning to sleep in tomorrow. Let's meet just outside the main gate at 7:30.

"And wear a comfortable pair of walking shoes."

BEHIND THE SCENES

Day 3, 7:25–8:15 A.M.

The next morning, everyone was at the main gate by 7:25. Alan and Carmen were in an animated discussion about market share. Bill was listening intently, adding an occasional comment or question from time to time. Judy was absorbed in her notebook, reviewing it page by page. And Don was looking around with at least the appearance of being interested.

Mort was thinking through how to position the final lesson. In some ways, it was the one lesson that made all the others work well or work poorly. He decided to start with a question.

"Bill, based on your experience here, which cast member would you say is more important—the one who helps you board the Jungle Cruise, the one who prepares your hamburger, the one who keeps the costumes in repair, the one who empties the trash cans, or the one who answers the phone at your hotel?"

"Well, the obvious answer is they're all important," Bill replied. "The place couldn't run without any one of them."

"How about at your bank?"

"Same thing. Everyone plays a part."

"Carmen?"

"I agree. The person who fills the order is just as important as the person who takes the call on the inside order desk, who's just as important as the person who deals with the manufacturer. . . . Everyone's important. Of course, they don't always feel important."

Everyone nodded in agreement, including Don.

"That's what I usually find in most companies. Here's my view on that issue," Mort said as he handed everyone a card bearing the following cryptic message:

LESSON 7

Xvxryonx makxs a diffxrxncx.

Puzzled by the strange spelling, Alan turned the card over. On the back he read:

> Somxtimxs I gxt to thinking that what I do doxsn't mattxr. But whxn I start thinking that way, I rxmxmbxr my old typxwritxr. Most of thx kxys workxd finx most of thx timx. But onx day, onx of thx kxys stoppxd working altogxthxr. And that rxally mxssxd xvxrything up. So whxn I'm txmptxd to say, I'm only onx pxrson, it won't makx much diffxrncx if I don't do this quitx right, I rxmxmbxr my old typxwritxr. And I say to mysxlf: "I am a kxy pxrson and nxxdxd vxry much."

Now, this I like, thought Alan. *This is the simplest and maybe the most powerful lesson of all.*

Mort waited for the group to finish reading. "Usually, I give some examples to help illustrate the lessons," he said, "but I've found that this lesson doesn't need any. The lesson says it all.

"It's usually helpful, though, for everyone in the group to talk about ways you can use this in your own company. How can you apply this lesson to do a better job of focusing on your customers? Any thoughts on that? Yes, Carmen?"

"First, I'd like to know, can I use this? I want to give it to every member of my team. In fact, I want to adapt it slightly, print up some cards, and give one to each person in the company."

"Yes, feel free to use it any way you see fit. All I ask is that you note the source. Just print 'Adapted from the book *Inside the Magic Kingdom*' and 'Used with the permission of the publisher' on the bottom of the card. I'm flattered you asked.

"Now, can you tell us how you expect this to help your company?"

Carmen smiled. "I'm thinking in particular of the people who pack the boxes, the people who send out invoices, the administrative staff. I'm thinking of my sales team. I'm thinking of everyone. To tell you the truth, I'm going to carry one with me. There are days when the whole world seems to be conspiring against me. Sometimes I feel like that guy—what's his name? Sisyphus?—who kept pushing the rock up the mountain, and when he got it to the top, it rolled down again. When that happens, I feel like what I do doesn't matter—even though in my heart of hearts, I know it does.

"So maybe the most immediate application is for me. But I think it would be good for everyone else, too."

"Good!" said Mort. He looked at the others.

Alan spoke next. "I'm going to include a version of this as part of my discussions with new employees. But first, I'm going to get it to all our current employees and see if I can start some silo busting. Any ideas, Mort?"

"My first thought," Mort said, "was to suggest doing it in natural workgroups, but now I'm thinking it might work even better to get together a cross section of people who don't normally work together. Might be an opportunity to do some team building and silo busting at the same time. It'll take a little longer, but if you have any teamwork problems between departments, this cross-functional approach will be time well spent."

"I keep hearing y'all throw around this word 'silo,'" smiled Judy. "Alan, you're in software, not farming. So tell me—what do *you* mean by 'silo'?"

"You're right, Judy. Farming's not my game," Alan laughed, "but we probably use 'silo' the same way you do. We use it to refer to people in a department who think only about their own departmental functions. They think and act up and down, rarely across the organization. For example, if accounting designs its systems to make it easy to crunch the numbers but ignores the impact on the customer or manufacturing, then accounting is acting like a silo. To achieve good teamwork and optimize customer loyalty, you have to break down the silos."

Judy nodded. "We use it the same way. There must be forty or fifty silos in our company that we could darn well get rid of! But that's not how I'm going to use this card, Mort. I'm going to use it with everyone on my team. And then I'm going to give one to

> **❝ To achieve good teamwork and optimize customer loyalty, you have to break down the silos. ❞**

everyone from information systems who comes over to help us maintain our equipment. They really do a great job, and we don't let them know often enough. It's the recognition thing you talked about yesterday. And I'll think of a lot more uses before I get home."

"I'm sure you will, Judy," said Mort. "Yes, Bill?"

"I'd love to be the one who distributes this throughout the bank," said Bill, "but I'm not going to. I think that would dilute the power of it. I'm going to take it up to the president. She supports this concept 100 percent. In fact, I can't think of anyone in a leadership position who doesn't believe in it. But coming from her rather than from me will increase its value immeasurably.

"I think it'll help us in two ways. First, it's a way of putting into very practical terms one of our corporate values: the importance of each employee's contribution. More important, perhaps, is that we have some people in the bank who espouse that belief but don't do very much to put it into practice. This may help them do a better job of walking the talk, as you so practically put it."

"Well said. How about you, Don?"

"Oh, I tell people all the time how important they are. But maybe this would help bring the message home in a different way. I'm not sure exactly how I'll use it, but I'm going to think about it."

"All good ideas," said Mort. "And now for our great lab experiment. Everybody got your safety goggles?"

Judy held up her Mickey Mouse ears, drawing a quick laugh from Carmen and Alan.

They were standing once more in front of City Hall.

"We've looked at seven key factors I've observed behind Disney's success," said Mort. "The competition is any business the customer compares you with; fantastic attention to detail; everyone walks the talk; everything walks the talk; multiple listening posts; reward, recognize, and celebrate; and everyone counts.

"I've tried to give you an outsider's view of how Disney puts these ideas into practice. You've probably thought about how they might apply to your company, and if you're like most people, some of them make more sense to you than others.

"Now I want you to do three things. First, sit down for ten or fifteen minutes and hold an imaginary conversation with yourself. Decide what lesson or lessons you understand the least or are least skilled at practicing. We like to call that your 'underdeveloped strength.'

"Then I'd like each of you to explore the Magic Kingdom on your own, concentrating on examples of that lesson or lessons. Don't ignore the other lessons, but concentrate on your underdeveloped strength. If you find examples you think would be of interest to the rest of the group, that's even better.

"Finally, I want you to develop a list of specific action steps you're going to take as a result of your time here. These items can be something you've already mentioned as a possibility, something you picked up from someone else in the group, or something that comes about as a result of your search.

"To help you in your journey around the Magic Kingdom, I have a special name badge and a letter of introduction for each of you, so that cast members and guests will feel comfortable talking to you."

Mort handed out the badges and letters. "It's now 7:55," he said. "That gives you about an hour to talk with cast members and see what goes on before things open. After that, take another five hours to see things in action. Visit attractions, watch cast members interact with guests, whatever. Just be sure to experience fully, observe closely, and take lots of notes.

"Then we'll meet back here at 2:00, and we'll talk and compare notes. Any questions?"

"I don't think it will take me a total of six hours to look around and finish taking notes," said Bill.

"Most of you probably won't take that long," agreed Mort, "but I want you to do more than observe what's going on in the Magic Kingdom. I also want you to observe what's going on in yourself. I want you to experience the experience. How are you reacting? What do you like, and why? What are the emotional components, and how do they fit into the overall picture?"

"Sounds reasonable," said Bill, "but what if two of us end up looking at the same thing?"

"Great!" replied Mort. "We'll have two different ways of looking at the same thing. The key thing is that you do what's important to you. Everyone learns something different. Remember that old saying, 'When the student is ready, the teacher will appear'? This is almost the same thing. Only it's 'When the student is ready, the lesson will appear.'

"So if two of you are looking at the same thing, and learning the same thing from it, that's what you were meant to learn. You could also look at the same thing and learn different but equally valuable lessons. Or you could look at two very different items and learn exactly the same thing. Concentrate on what you're learning, not on whether you're doing it right or wrong."

Alan spoke up. "Do we have to limit ourselves to the Magic Kingdom?" he asked. "We focused most of our attention here, but we also looked at some of the hotels."

"How about if we agree that you'll limit yourselves to anything we've talked about or physically visited, or that guests or cast members happen to bring up in your discussions with them?"

The Gang of Five agreed.

"Great! Let's plan on meeting back here at 2:00. Happy hunting!"

As Judy wandered alone, she pondered the paradox of the Magic Kingdom. Clearly, Disney World was magical. She could feel it. Everywhere she looked there was magic. The voices of cast members and guests all had a magical lilt. So there was no doubt that this Kingdom really was Magic.

But apparently it didn't just happen by magic. It wasn't as if someone waved a wand and suddenly everything appeared.

She reviewed the cards Mort had given her so far.

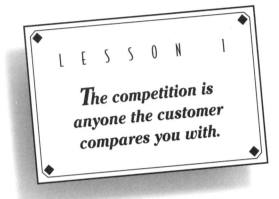

L E S S O N 1

The competition is anyone the customer compares you with.

The first lesson was a new thought for Judy, but it made sense. People did call FedEx, they did call her company, and they did call L. L. Bean. Sure, they'd compare all those calls. And people called Disney, too. Judy didn't like to think of Disney World as a competitor. But the park did so many things so well that guests would expect other companies—including hers—to match the same high standards.

People at work had been saying how competitive things were, but no one said exactly why. Judy didn't think any of them had thought about Mort's first lesson. She resolved to point it out to her staff and colleagues.

Then Judy pulled up the second card Mort had given everyone.

This was the one that most puzzled her—all this planning and attention to detail. Cast members went to any length to make each guest's experience truly magical. The director of marketing she reported to kept talking about "execution." "We've got to execute, execute, execute!" was his favorite saying, followed closely by "The devil is in the details."

Judy understood the lesson in her head, but her heart didn't really buy into it. Maybe she'd find the rest of the connection somewhere else. So she turned to the third card.

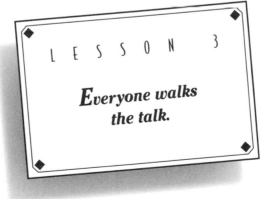

Judy really liked this one. She believed it whole-heartedly. Of course, the president of her company wasn't as strong on it. He kept talking about "the importance of customers," but he didn't do much to back it up. In fact, what he said and what he did were sometimes two very different things. She wished he would come to hear what Mort had to say about *everyone* walking the talk.

She also wished the president could hear Mort talk about the next lesson.

L E S S O N   4

*Everything walks
the talk.*

A lot of things in her company didn't walk the talk. No one expected gold-leaf paint or anything like that. But there was a lot that could be done, for little or no money, that would make things work and feel better.

As for the next two lessons, Judy liked them both. She looked at the card in her left hand.

L E S S O N 5

Customers are best heard through many ears.

What a great idea! Sometimes she felt as though she and her staff were the only people in the company responsible for customer loyalty. My gosh! Everyone should be responsible for customer loyalty. Sales, accounting, dispatch—everyone! Certainly she and her team were responsible for a lot of customer contact, but many other employees learned things that, if Judy and her staff had only known them, could have vastly improved customer service. Those employees should hear this lesson.

Then Judy looked at the card in her right hand.

L E S S O N 6

Reward, recognize, and celebrate.

Of all the lessons, Judy liked this one best, maybe because she was naturally good at recognizing and celebrating. The pizza parties with her team were great; they pulled everyone together. Mark, one of the people she had worried about most when she took over customer service, had pulled a stack of her "way-to-go's" out of his drawer one day and told her how they had pulled him through some tough days.

And the annual opinion survey always ranked her high in this area. Most people specifically mentioned the "What Our Boss, the Customer, Says" bulletin board she had set up as a motivator. So on this one, Judy was with Mort all the way. It was her favorite.

Except, perhaps, for the last lesson—

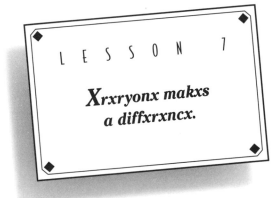

L E S S O N 7

Xrxryonx makxs a diffxrxncx.

How could anything top that?

Now she was more confused than ever. Where should she do her "lab work"? Out of all these lessons, which one represented her most underdeveloped strength? She understood most of them, liked some better than others, but felt she had something to learn in all of them. Perhaps the lesson on attention to detail was the one she should concentrate on.

Somehow, though, she couldn't work up any enthusiasm for it—she who was so good at enthusiasm. She loved Disney World. She wanted to visit the whole place all over again, to wander through it and enjoy its magic, just as she had done before with her family. Just as she had done when she first dreamed about—

Suddenly Judy knew what she was going to do.

Don strolled down Main Street at a leisurely pace, a bit relieved to be away from Mort and the others. People with too much undirected energy made him tired. Mort made him tired. Sure, some of what he said made sense, but a lot of it you had to take on faith.

It was all entirely too irrational. You couldn't tension a heartstring; you couldn't put a caliper to touchy-feely. *Fanatical obsession with meaningless detail,* he thought. *Pixie Dust, my royal red elbow,* he thought.

He'd heard it all before in his company. We're All One Big Happy Family. Empower Everyone. Team Spirit. They all came and went, and everything was like it was before.

Let's try to look at it rationally, he thought. He walked over to a bench, a little away from the stream of visitors, and sat down. All that fuzzy conceptual stuff. It was there, and yet it was not there. It was present underneath, but missing on the surface.

There *was* a family feel. Kind of a good one, too. But no one proclaiming it. The place was fun and pretty magical—even for him. But no T-shirts with slogans. And this empowerment stuff. No one had mentioned the word, but the Disney employees—*okay, cast members*—acted just the way his boss's favorite guru—*excuse me, consultant*—had said empowered people should act.

An irrational notion: *What would my CEO do if some line worker walked up to him and said, "Excuse me, but your name tag is missing!"? Come to think of it, how would I react? Maybe the boss wasn't walking the talk. Maybe I'm not either,* he thought.

Team spirit here? Absolutely. Employees shouting, "Go, team, go!"? Not a chance. Big posters proclaiming love for customers—uh, guests? Nope.

Something about this place works, he thought. *Cast members really do seem to care about the guests. They do it without posters and slogans. They do it for a letter and a photo on the bulletin board.* He thought again of his last quarter. The way he'd anticipated his boss's appreciation. And then nothing. *One lousy compliment wouldn't have killed him,* Don thought. Then he pulled himself up short.

Enough of this nonsense, he thought. *Now—how can I waste the next six hours enjoyably?*

He looked around at all the smiling faces.

Well, I could do what I used to do when I was a kid: sit with a note pad and count things as they go by. Ice cream wagons. Mouse ears. Balloons. What should it be?

Suddenly he remembered something Carmen had said about the number twelve. He flipped back to what he'd written. Ha! He could have fun, and at the same time. . . .

SILO BUSTING
MADE EASY

Day 3, 1:55–2:15 P.M.

At five minutes before the appointed time, the Gang of Five, minus Don, was standing in front of City Hall, trading tall tales. "I had lunch in France with Donald Duck!" Alan said.

"Forget France. I dined in Japan with Goofy and Minnie," Judy boasted.

They turned as Mort walked up. Judy asked, "Where'd you have lunch, Mort?"

"Just about everywhere," he said, and held up the remains of a cheese sandwich. "Where's Don?"

"Just around the corner, I think," said Carmen. "I saw him crouched down talking with some little girl." She waited before adding, "At least, it looked like Don."

Judy laughed. "Now, Carmen, be nice."

"Here he comes," whispered Alan.

Don walked up briskly at 2:01, slightly out of breath, pencil in one hand, open note pad in the other. "Sorry I'm late."

"You're right on time," said Mort. "Okay, folks, I know you've just finished a lot of hard work. Now comes the fun part. Let's find a shady spot and tell each other stories."

Mort looked at the group seated around him. He said, "This is the part where we stand up and tell each other about our observations and insights. Since you've undoubtedly spent most of the last six hours on your feet, you can stay seated if you like. Take five, ten, fifteen minutes, as long as you need. Everybody else, feel free to ask questions.

"Now, I know everyone's eager to go first, so to avoid offending anybody, I've already worked out the most logical order. The first presenter will be the person with the smallest notebook."

The Gang of Five looked down at their note pads, then at their neighbors'. All eyes turned to Don, who, after a pause, closed his tiny leather book and said, "I'd rather go last."

"Well," said Mort, one eyebrow raised, "that puts us in a bind, because the next person on the list is whoever starts talking first."

"I'll go," said Bill.

"You've got the floor," said Mort.

"I haven't had time to organize this," Bill began, "so I'll just go down my list in the order that I made the notes. Hope it makes sense by the end." He thumbed through several pages.

"Actually, the first thing is something I noticed while I was thinking about what to look for.

"I was sitting on a bench and there was a T-shaped post nearby. Each part of the T had a plant hanging down. I was admiring how attractive the design was and how healthy the plants looked. All of a sudden, the plants were being watered. I saw that each arm of the T had a small sprinkler built into it. Everything about that planter had been thought out in advance, down to the tiniest detail—the symmetrical design, the cost savings from not having to water by hand, and so on.

"But that was just a point of interest. After the sprinkler went off eleven minutes later—out of curiosity, I timed it—I decided, what I wanted to look into was the contribution of individual cast members. I wanted to see how everyone plays an important role.

"I stopped a cast member who was walking by, showed her my letter, and asked her if she had a couple of minutes to talk. She said sure. I asked her how important she considered her role and in what ways she felt supported in that role. I assured her I wouldn't reveal her name.

"She told me that over the past week she had renewed her driver's license and gotten a mammogram—right here at Disney World. She also said that you could buy stamps, get your hair done at any of several hair salons and barbershops, even buy shoes from the shoemobile—all right here. She said that although such services might seem unimportant to some people, they meant a lot to her. They saved her a lot of time and made life easier. They also told her that she was important.

"Then she pulled out a card that she called 'Donald's ID.' A cast member can use this to get discounts at restaurants, movie theaters, rock concerts, and sporting events, sometimes even tickets to special events that might otherwise be impossible to get into.

"But, she said, the best thing is the support she feels from other cast members. She told me about her friendship with Pat, a cast member and teammate. Sometimes when things work out just right, she said, she and Pat look at each other and say, 'No place but here.' She really likes the way everybody pulls together."

"I wonder how long she'd been working here when she first started feeling that way," said Judy.

"Not long, I think. She's been here seven years, I think she said, but she still remembers her first Traditions sessions, the stories about Walt and other Disney people, the feeling of being in on things from the start—part of a team, not just a cog in a machine, as she put it.

"And I got the sense from her that her idea of teamwork included working with cast members at Resorts. That's what they call the hotels. This part is called Parks, right, Mort? She didn't seem to have the attitude,

'I'm from Parks and she's in Resorts'—that us-and-them thing you see in so many places—including my bank.

"It reminded me of something that happened at the office just last week. I was talking with one of our customers, an entrepreneur who's fanatical about customer service. During our conversation she happened to mention that she didn't feel like a customer of our bank. She felt like a customer of the checking department, a customer of the commercial loans department, a customer of the mortgage department. There wasn't any one person who represented the bank. And when communication was required between departments, they dropped the ball. I'm not sure yet what I can do about that, but I'm going to tackle it as soon as I get back. No one should feel that way. Dealing with our bank should be an absolutely seamless experience."

"The silo effect strikes again," said Judy. Alan nodded.

Bill continued. "So anyway—the park was about to open and the cast member had work to do, so I decided to go out and come back in to experience it the way most guests do. I was glad I did. I got to see how even the ticket taker can brighten a guest's day from the start.

"I was in line just behind a group of four women. As the gatekeeper took one of the women's ticket, she said, 'Welcome back, Mary!' The woman lit up with a big smile and went on in.

"I stayed near the group for a minute or so, eaves-dropping. Mary was amazed and pleased that the gate person had remembered her name. She wondered how she could possibly have done it, with so many visitors coming through all the time.

"Mary's friends pointed out that she was wearing earrings with her name on them. 'Oh, that's right,' she said. But how did the girl know that she had been here before? It had been a year since her last visit.

"I doubled back and asked the ticket taker. Simple, she said. She *had* noticed the earrings. She also knew that 70 percent of all guests are repeat guests, so the odds were in her favor that Mary was, too. But what tipped the scale was intuition—just a feeling, a hunch that Mary had visited before.

"I was amazed. This young person had used a sophisticated combination of attention to detail, background knowledge, intuition, and what you could only call 'aggressive friendliness' and, in a split second, immeasurably brightened one customer's day. I wish we could send all our people here to watch her do her job. Especially our drive-up tellers."

"They'll have to get in line behind my technical support staff," said Carmen.

"And my mother-in-law," said Judy. Everybody laughed.

Bill went on. "But let me tell you about the next cast member I ran into. I was talking with him when a couple with three kids came up and asked him—get this—what time the 3:00 parade started. I'm thinking to myself, *How much dumber can a question be?*

"But the cast member's reaction surprised me. And, I'll have to admit, humbled me. He smiled at them and said, 'Well, the parade *does* start on time, and you should get there around 2:30 to get a really good place.' The couple thanked him and walked on.

"As I thought about it, I realized he didn't answer the question they asked. He did something even better. He answered their unasked question—what they really wanted to know. That's a very special skill. And it's a good attitude—believing people are smarter than they sometimes seem, knowing that people sometimes have trouble saying things clearly. It's an attitude I wish more people in the bank had."

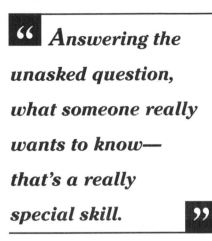

" *Answering the unasked question, what someone really wants to know— that's a really special skill.* "

"Wow, Bill," Judy exclaimed, "you know who that cast member sounds like? Did you ever watch *M*A*S*H*, the movie or the TV show? Do you remember Radar O'Reilly? He could always hear the choppers coming before anybody else. And he always knew what Colonel Blake wanted even before the colonel knew.

"I think when I get back I'll create a Radar O'Reilly Award for people who do an outstanding job of *anticipating* either an internal or external customer's needs."

"Not a bad idea," said Bill. "We could certainly use an idea like that in the bank. It would help us do a better job of holding onto the customers we want. Can I borrow it?"

"Sure. Just say, 'Used by permission of Judy Crawford, Customer Service and TV Reruns Freak'!"

Then Judy noticed that everyone was hurriedly scribbling notes—including Mort. "Mort!" she said. "You're taking down what I'm saying?"

"Hey, I get to learn, too!" said Mort. "That's why I like conducting these sessions. Every time I do, I get new ideas to share with the next group. Let's see . . . 'Used by permission of. . . .' Is that the way you said it?"

"All right, I'm taking over this class," she said. "I want to hear what else Bill has to say."

Bill laughed. "You know," he said, "if we had this much fun at the bank, half our customer problems would be solved overnight.

"That's one of the things I realized when I set out this morning. I know one of my underdeveloped strengths has to do with fun. I tend to be a pretty sober guy at work. It's partly the way banks are, because bankers think customers don't have confidence in bankers who laugh a lot.

"But it's me, as well. I probably don't get out and have as much fun as I should. Sometimes I think my grandchildren are afraid of me. I spend a lot of time with serious things. Every year since I graduated, I have mentored a recent graduate from my college. I take that and most everything else I do very seriously.

"So this morning I decided to go looking for fun things. It wasn't anything we'd talked about, yet we're surrounded by it here. I thought I'd try to imagine myself a child again and do something only a child could fully appreciate. And what's more fun for a child than to visit It's a Small World?

"So I went there. And even though I'm no longer a child, I enjoyed it. Wished the whole time I'd had the grandkids here, but promised myself that I'd bring them later.

"As you know, the attraction is full of dolls from all over the world. And I learned something particularly interesting about that—something a cast member told me: there are only two United States dolls there.

"Now, I'm as patriotic as the next person, but I rather liked that. Sometimes in our mainstream culture we tend to put on blinders and think that the U.S. is everything. Maybe as an African-American, I'm more aware of that than most.

"I left there feeling good. I was hungry, too, so I decided on lunch in the Moroccan Pavilion at Epcot.

"I found myself standing in line next to a former cast member, so I invited him to eat with me. The food was excellent, and so was the conversation. I learned that although the basic design of the Moroccan Pavilion was done by the Imagineers, the artwork and decoration were hand-crafted by twenty-three palace artisans from Morocco. In six months, they created the fountains, artwork, and many other beautiful objects. Their work was a gift to Disney.

"The tiles are the same as those used to decorate palaces in Morocco. The artwork uses no images of plant, animal, or human life. Islam forbids the representation—in art—of living things, so all the designs are geometric patterns.

"I also learned that the whole showcase was inspired by three cities—Fez, Casablanca, and Marrakech. So it's not just the tiles—the whole design 'walks the talk' of three different cities. And just like most Moroccan cities, the showcase is divided into two sections—the Villa Nouvelle or new city, and the Medina, the old city.

"My last note is about some of those little details that catch your attention and just make you feel good," Bill went on. "I had a little time left, so on my way back here I meandered down Main Street. I happened to look up, and there was this 'business' on the second story—Turkish Baths. And it says Dick Nunis, Supervisor. Nunis? Oh, yes, the chairman of Disney Attractions, I remembered. And there's also a gym named for him.

"Then I started looking at the names above all the stores. Some of them didn't ring a bell, so I asked a cast member to explain them. Here's some of what I found:

"M. T. Lott Real Estate Investments. That's a nice pun, of course, but the subsidiaries listed beneath—Latin American Development, Tomahawk Properties,

Ayefour Corporation, Compass East Corporation, Reedy Creek Ranch, and Bay Lake Properties—those are the fictitious companies created to purchase the land for Disney World before the location of the park was made public.

"Then there's Roy E. Disney, Sailmaker and Sailing Lessons. That's over the Crystal Arts store. Roy E. is Walt's nephew. His father, Roy O. Disney, oversaw the building of Disney World following Walt's death. They also have Patty Disney, Roy E.'s wife, listed in that company and then four names I assume are their children—Susan, Timothy, Roy Patrick, and Abigail.

"Ron and Diane Miller's Lazy M Cattle Company of Wyoming appears over the Bakery Shop where we've had coffee each morning. Ron is a former chairman of the Walt Disney Company, and Diane is one of Walt's daughters. Their children are listed as partners in the business.

"But the best one for me was Walter E. Disney's Ice Cream Corner. That's Walt, of course, but out of all those names, Walt's is the only one that faces Cinderella Castle. To me, that's special, the same way the gold-leaf paint on the carousel is special.

"Most of these are things only a cast member would know or recognize. Maybe they're each just small, seemingly inconsequential, inside jokes. But string them all together, and they become significant. The same thing holds true at my bank. Put several seemingly inconsequential things together, and all of a sudden they become something significant.

"Now—Mort, you said to pay attention also to what was going on inside us. The main thing I noticed was about fun. Disney's a fun place—fun for kids of all ages. For cast members. For everyone. Even for bank officers.

"Sometimes I confuse being serious about what I do with taking myself too seriously. So I'm going to try to have more fun doing what I do at the bank, but not at the expense of being any less serious about fulfilling my responsibilities."

"Outstanding!" said Mort. "I liked your examples of attention to detail and walking the talk, and you were very forthcoming about underdeveloped strengths—although judging from what I can see, I think you underestimated yourself. Now, did you come up with any specific ideas about how to use these insights at your bank?"

"Well, as I've said, first I'm going to use Judy's Radar O'Reilly idea.

"Next, I'm going to call back the woman who didn't feel like a customer of the bank. I'm going to ask her to join me in a meeting with several bank officers, including representatives of the functions she dealt with. There's real value in hearing something straight from the customer. I'm going to ask her to give it to us straight. What happened? What could have prevented it? How should we do things in the future? Then we're going to act on what she says. We've got customer satisfaction surveys all over the place, but individuals like this woman are an overlooked listening post that we need to tap. And we're going to tap it! I'm going to look for more customers like her. The more listening posts, the better. Fewer surveys and more listening!

"I was also inspired by the importance of Traditions and by the shop names on Main Street. Most of our employees don't think about tradition, aren't even aware of our roots. I want to find some way to build more tradition into our employee orientation —if possible, with a twist of humor. We've got a long history in our community, clear back to the early '20s. And while we have some great old photographs of the early days, they're all in the boardroom—the people who really count rarely see them. We might create an interesting public display out of those. Maybe just for fun we could celebrate Founders' Day on our anniversary, dress up in old-fashioned clothes for the day, hand out certificates for five-cent hamburgers or something else to buy at a 1920s price.

❝ *There's real value in hearing something straight from the customer.* ❞

"I'm going to push for more attention to detail, too. Not in financial things—we pay an enormous amount of attention to detail there. Where we fall short is in the details of customer focus. Part of every training session should be about customer satisfaction and retention. Not just customer rep training, but commercial loan officer orientation, computer training, and all other areas as well.

"Finally, I'm going to stop banking at our main branch. I'm going to do my banking at one of the other branches. Everything is pretty easy for me, and especially at the main branch, but that may not be true for other customers. If I can experience our bank the way our customers experience it, I'll probably gain a whole new perspective on what our customers might think."

With that, Bill folded his notebook.

"Well done," said Mort. "You gave us exactly the kind of report I asked for. I'll bet you're a tough act to follow in board meetings."

"Tough to follow here, too," said Carmen. "But if he's using Judy's idea, I guess I'm entitled to use his. I've got two fresh pages of notes here. And I'm not the only one."

"That's what this is all about," said Mort. "If you're going to take your business to the next level, you can't do it all by yourself. Ideas don't care who has them, and they don't care where they come from. They just care that they're used. Go for it!"

HOW DISNEY PICKS
THE RIGHT PEOPLE

Day 3, 2:15–2:30 P.M.

"**L**et's see," said Mort, glancing down at his notebook. "The next presenter will be the person with the biggest ears."

They looked at each other. "Oh, yeah," said Judy. She dug into her purse and popped the big, round ears on her head.

"You had me worried," said Alan. "I wasn't quite ready." The others laughed while Judy opened her notebook.

"Okay," said Judy. "First of all, it's no secret that I think Disney World is a terrific place. I've been excited for weeks just thinking about coming here.

"But what I haven't ever told anyone is that one of my dreams has always been to become a cast member.

I've been here three times before now, and each time I've had this secret urge to apply for work.

"So that's what I decided to do this morning. What better time to see if my dreams could come true? So that's what I did."

"Now, that's walking the talk!" exclaimed Alan.

"You applied for a job here?" asked Mort.

"I sure did! Of course, I felt a little guilty about it because I knew I wouldn't really ever take it. After all, I've got a great job, and I'm not about to ask my family to pull up roots and move down here. But I've always wondered, and I wanted to see if I could make the grade. Know what I mean?"

"Yes, I think I do," said Mort. "So what happened?"

"Well, I went up to a cast member and asked her where I could find out about working here. She gave me directions—and when she pointed out where I needed to go, I noticed that she pointed with two fingers instead of just one. Like this." She demonstrated. "Now, I saw you do that the other day, Mort, and I thought it was kind of odd, but I didn't think any more about it until I saw her do it too.

"So I asked her what's with the double digits. She said there were two reasons. First, it's a little easier to keep your arm straight with two fingers, so it's easier to tell where you're pointing. Try it."

They tried one- and two-finger points and agreed that two was better.

"The other reason," said Judy, "is that in some cultures pointing with one finger is considered impolite or even insulting. It's just a little detail, but it's an important one.

"Anyway, I arrived at Central Casting. Oh, and the reason it's called casting is because you are not hired here, you are cast for a role. Another example of everything walking the talk. The first thing I noticed was a brass caterpillar-head doorknob, straight out of *Alice in Wonderland.* I had this rush like I was a little girl again, going to see the movie for the first time.

"I remembered what you said about everything walking the talk, Mort. That doorknob is really a good example. Few guests will ever see it—that's not who it's there for. It's there for potential cast members. I wonder how many of them see that doorknob and remember the movie and have the same nostalgia rush I did. I'll bet that really adds to the magic of working here.

"I began to understand then just how all the little things add up. I mean, Mort, I thought I understood what you were telling us before, but after I saw that *Alice in Wonderland* doorknob, I *really* began to know it. Later one of the cast members told me that the doorknob was there to put applicants at ease and show them how everything walks the talk. So I guess it did exactly what it was designed to do. It worked on me!

"I decided I'd better take off my badge so people wouldn't ask why a special guest was applying to work here. Then I went on in. I walked down a hallway and into a rotunda lined with statues of Disney characters. I noticed that all of them had gold paint—just like the carousel you told us about. I wouldn't know the difference, so I'm assuming that must have been 23-karat gold-leaf paint, too. I've got to say, Mort, that your talks with us sure helped me see all those details. I'd probably have missed them on my own.

"Anyway, I talked to the receptionist and told him I wanted to apply. I didn't know what to expect, but there were a lot of other applicants there already, and right away they put a bunch of us in a room and showed us a short videotape. It told all about the basic conditions of employment and things like that.

"It was pretty straightforward about the high standards Disney expected cast members to uphold. The person running the session told us that after watching the video we might feel that being a Disney World cast member was just what we wanted, or maybe that it wasn't right for us. He said that if we didn't feel there was a good fit, there'd be no hard feelings if we decided not to go ahead.

"And you know what? Out of about twenty-five of us, four people got up and left right after the video. At first I was put off by that, but then I realized it just made good sense. This isn't the place for everyone. You may be very talented, you may be a genius, but if you have to work hard to keep a smile on your face, you'll probably go crazy here. The video helped some people select themselves out before they wasted their time, and Disney's, in interviews.

"I stayed, and right away I was called into the interview which lasted about thirty minutes."

Judy fell silent. The others looked at her.

"And?" asked Carmen.

Judy smiled. "I got it."

"They offered you a job?" asked Bill.

"They sure did!"

"Way to go, Judy!" said Mort. "But you said—"

"Yeah, of course I couldn't take it, Mort. I told them I felt a bit guilty about the whole thing, wasting their time and all, so as soon as they offered me a job, I let them know right off that I couldn't really take it, I was just doing research. I showed them my letter and badge. I told them where I worked and what I did. I also said I'd like to find out more about their screening and hiring methods.

"I said I felt honored to be offered a position, especially since I've learned so much in the last three days about what it takes to be a good cast member. They weren't upset at all, and they said they'd be glad to let me continue through the process. They even seemed pleased that I was interested in how they did things. That made me feel better.

"The next step was a benefits briefing. The interviewer was about to take a break, so he offered to spend it with me explaining the entire process. Here's what he told me.

"At the end of the interview, one of three things can happen. One, you get an offer. Two, you're told you're not a very strong candidate right now and they list the reasons. Three, you're told you're a very strong candidate but there are no positions now and can they call you back.

"The interviewers are there on rotation for nine to twelve months, and collectively they interview 75,000 people a year.

"Then comes the training. First is Traditions, which we all know about. But that's just the beginning. After Traditions, the training you get depends on whether you're going into Resorts or Parks or whatever. That's a more specialized kind of training.

"Then, new cast members get three to five days of individual training. After that is a check-out verification. That's where the trainer decides whether the new cast member needs more training before going 'on stage.' The last thing they want is someone on stage who's not ready."

"That's a lot of training," said Bill, looking at Mort.

"It is," acknowledged Mort, "but it's also critical. For every hundred dollars in compensation, world-class companies invest five or six dollars in training. My experience has been that companies that grow people grow profits. Companies that shrink people shrink profits. So look at the investment in human assets your company is making to be sure it's enough."

"There's even more," Judy said as she leafed through her notebook. "Oh, Bill? You were talking about that ticket taker? This will interest you. Ticket Taking and Selling is a two-week course. Two weeks! No wonder that cast member knew to say 'Welcome back, Mary.'

"And listen to this! The cast member I was talking to used to be in Guest Relations. The course for Guest Relations is also two weeks. But here's the killer. He said the test for that two-week course is four to six hours long and that it was tougher than his constitutional law exams in college. Now, that's tough!

" *Companies that grow people, grow profits. Companies that shrink people, shrink profits.* "

"There's more training for experienced cast members. During Career Enhancement Week you can take a class called Future Careers that tells you about new opportunities that are going to open in Disney World and how to prepare for them."

Judy flipped page after page in her notebook. "There are courses on interviewing—how to put together a good résumé, how to use your résumé to sell yourself, how to interview the interviewer. There's a class on how to transfer, how to talk with your supervisor about going up further in the organization.

"Then there's a class called Wish upon a Star—kind of a motivational class. It gives you more about the history of Walt Disney. About his dreams. And how your dreams are important. It also shows you the difference you can make. It helps each cast member see how he or she is part of the stage production.

"But the training program that I liked best was We've Come a Long Way, Mickey. This is for people who've been cast members for a long time but haven't had a good opportunity to get out and see how things have changed. Maybe they've added two resorts, five restaurants, and three attractions since you went through Traditions. You're taken off the job for three days of classes, a lot of which you spend touring the park to see what's new and different. It's education, but it's also R and R—a chance to revitalize yourself, to avoid burnout.

> **" *Loyal customers are not the result of happy accidents.* "**

"Train, train, train. I sound like Johnny Cash, don't I? But I guess what I'm trying to say is that I made a pass at my longtime dream of becoming a cast member, and I learned plenty about how much training goes into being a good cast member. It was a real eye-opener for me.

"When I got here, I just assumed that people were hired and given a day or two of orientation and then assigned to whatever job needed filling at the moment. You know, hire good people and turn 'em loose to do their thing. But I found out there's an awful lot of planning and training and hard work that goes into making sure each guest has a great time.

"If I had to cut a long story short—something we Southerners are not known for—I'd say that happy guests are not the result of happy accidents."

Alan and Carmen were scribbling furiously, trying to keep up.

"No, let me say it the way I would for my company: Loyal customers are not the result of happy accidents. They are the result of detailed planning, seamless teamwork, and flawless execution. How's that?"

"That's great, Judy," said Mort. "Now can you tell us how you plan to translate that into action?"

"Well, I've been pretty busy listening and learning, but, yeah, I've thought of a few things. . . .

"I've always looked at the people part of the equation and almost never at systems. I figured you could motivate people to do anything. But now I see that you need systems to support them right from the start.

"So the first thing I'm going to do is revamp the way we hire our customer service reps. I've always hired them by interviewing them face to face. As I was walking around today, I realized that our customers never experience our CSRs face to face. They experience them over the phone. Now, some people might make a good impression face to face but not be so good over the phone. So from now on, my first interview with everyone is going to be over the phone. That way, I can experience the applicant the same way a customer might.

"I'll still interview them face to face, of course, because there are things you can find out in a face-to-face interview you'll never find out over the phone. But I'm going to use the phone interview as a first pass.

"I also tried to think of some questions I could ask that would give me a better idea of how people might actually behave. I've been asking standard questions and getting pat answers. Here are some of the new questions I came up with."

Judy cleared her throat and read them to the group.

Has there ever been a time when a customer asked for something unreasonable? How did you handle it?

I know I sometimes get uptight when I have to deal with an irate customer. You've had experience with difficult customers. How did you handle them?

Tell me about a time when you went beyond the call of duty in taking care of a customer.

When you came here today, what did you notice about our customer service that we do well? Where do we need to improve?

What do you like most about being in a customer contact position?

What do you like *least* about being in a customer contact position?

She looked at her friends and said, "Here's a really good one." She continued,

> Now and then we all get weary of the pressure of meeting the public. How do you stay up, fresh, and enthusiastic? How do you deal with the stress of customer contact?

Judy covered her notes with her hand and added, "I figure there aren't any pat answers to those. People have to give me real answers to real-life situations they're going to face on the job. I bet there are hundreds of good questions like these I could ask, but that's a start."

"It's a *great* start!" exclaimed Carmen. "Could I get a copy of that list?"

"Sure, I'll get it typed up when I get home and send you a copy." She looked at the others. "Anyone else want one?"

Five heads nodded yes—including Mort's and Don's.

"You got it," said Judy. "By the way, I haven't got all of your business cards yet. And here's mine." She handed everybody a card.

"Another thing I'm going to start doing is pre-recruiting people. I've got a friend back home who carries extra business cards with him everywhere. When someone gives him good service, whether it's in a restaurant, a grocery store, or the dry cleaner's, my friend gives him his card, tells him he's always looking for good people, and says if he's ever looking for a job to give him a call. He says he gets some of his best people that way. I'm going to try the same thing.

"So those are the things I'm going to do, based on what I learned about the way Disney hires. Naturally I'm not going to do the same thing Disney does, because our needs aren't the same. But I'm going to build the idea of systems into the way we hire.

"And I was really impressed with the amount of training that goes on here. We do some, and it's good, but there's so much more we could do. So I'm going to develop some ideas for more training. Some of it will be regular training and some will be informal.

"For example, I'm going to get a team of eight to ten customer service reps together once a week and ask them to talk about how they handled their toughest phone calls. They're on the front line of customer contact every day, and I know they run into tough situations, and I know they handle them. But we never share that knowledge they have or build it into the way we do business. How our best people handle tough situations never gets written down. We need to start doing that.

"Next, I'm going to start looking at other systems. If Disney can use laptops to interview people, then there have got to be ways we can do a better job of using technology. The information systems people have been pestering me about something they call middleware. I've never really made the effort to understand it. But I will."

"Middleware is—" Alan began, but Judy didn't even slow down.

"I'm also going to put special emphasis on the lesson about who the competition is. As everyone knows, utilities are taking a wild ride with all this deregulation and new kinds of competition. We keep talking about the importance of customer service because it's the only thing that really differentiates us from someone else. But it never occurred to me that the standard is being set by companies outside our industry. I have to get that message through to everyone."

She waited for their response, but everyone was silent. "So I guess that's all," she laughed. "Oh, I almost forgot. I've decided I'm going to trademark the Radar O'Reilly Award."

KEEPING CUSTOMERS WHO COUNT

Day 3, 2:30–2:45 P.M.

"Thanks, Judy," said Mort. "Well, folks, I seem to have misplaced my agenda and I can't remember who's the next speaker. It's either the tallest person wearing earrings or the shortest person wearing a top hat."

Carmen blushed, touched her ear, and smiled. "Well, this may sound odd, but I really liked the Hall of Presidents, and I was still thinking about it, so after we split up I went back there.

"I looked around, found a cast member, and introduced myself. I showed her my letter and told her about what we were doing. I didn't have anything specific to ask her, I just wanted to know more about the place. She said she'd be happy to help.

"These are some of the things I found out.

"First, the people in Imagineering spent more than fifteen years on the concept, design, and execution of the Hall of Presidents. Two research librarians worked full time for eighteen months and came up with more than 600 books, 300 magazines, and 5,000 photographs to be used as reference material.

"When we were there before, I was impressed by what you said about the stitching, Mort. But that's just a drop in the bucket compared to everything else. George Washington's chair, for instance. It's an exact replica of the chair he sat in during the Constitutional Convention in 1787.

"But even more than that, I liked Franklin D. Roosevelt. I guess everybody knows he was paralyzed and wore leg braces, but most people don't usually think about that. The Hall of Presidents has him seated in a chair. Lift the trouser cuff and you can see that he's wearing a full set of braces. Now, they could have left out that detail and not a single guest would know. But that just reaffirmed two lessons for me—attention to detail and everything walks the talk.

"Then I remembered our visit to the castle, and that raised more questions in my mind. So I went back there, too, to look for more examples of attention to detail. I discovered several interesting little facts. For one thing, the mosaic mural took six people almost two years to complete. There are hundreds of thousands of pieces of glass in it. Some of them are even fused together with 14-karat gold and silver.

"The best thing, though, was something a lot like the business names that Bill found on Main Street— Nunis's Gym and so forth. The castle has crests representing the families of the people who actually helped Walt Disney. There's the Nunis family coat of arms, the Lund family—Sharon Disney Lund is one of Walt's daughters. Then there's the Redmond Family; Dorthea Redmond is the designer of the mosaic.

"I was having fun discovering the significance of all these details. I told the cast member—his name was Tim—about the other hidden details we had talked about, and asked him if there were any other 'fun' things around Disney World that might not be apparent to the average guest.

"T im's eyes twinkled as he answered my question. 'There's some neat stuff over at the Haunted Mansion,' he said, and offered to walk me over there. On the way, he gave me some background on that attraction. Walt wanted a haunted house but didn't want a building that looked run down. For the right look, he decided on a southern mansion. He had said, 'We'll keep up the grounds and things outside, and the ghosts can take care of the inside.'

"To help the ghosts maintain the run-down look of the Haunted Mansion, Disney World buys a special 'dust' by the pound and lays it down with a fertilizer spreader. Since it opened, they've spread enough dust to bury the entire mansion.

"When we got to the mansion, Tim showed me where the designers had had fun with the details. For instance, there's a group of tombstones outside the mansion. The names on them are those of the Imagineers who helped create the attraction. I copied them down."

Carmen began to read from her notebook. "'Grandpa Marc' is Marc Davis. He's the art director who did most of the concept design for the attraction.

"'A Man Named Martin' is Bud Martin, former head of the Special Effects Department.

"'Brother Dave.' That's Dave Burkhart, the art director who helped build models of the Haunted Mansion.

"'Wathel Bender' is really Wathel Rogers. Around here he's called the Grandfather of Audio-Animatronics. That's the technology of making inanimate objects move like living things. It's what makes Lincoln move and talk.

"So, anyway, after I'd been wandering around and gathering all these little intriguing details for a while, I realized that I hadn't even thought about my under-developed strengths. So I was not really following the spirit of your assignment, Mort. I was not being very structured about this task, and that surprised me when I thought about it, because I'm usually very structured.

"So what *was* I doing? I was just drifting around, looking for things that interested me. I was relaxed. I was having fun. I was learning a lot of things.

"That's when it struck me—my underdeveloped strength. It's a lot like what you said, Bill. We don't have enough fun in my company.

"I began to realize that building a little fun into the work is a way to make the work go smoother, to get people to interact better, to put people in a relaxed frame of mind so they can learn things more easily. Just the way I was doing here.

> **❝ *It's more important to acquire the customers who count than to count the customers you acquire.* ❞**

"That really seems to be what's going on here. Every cast member I've met seems to take her job very seriously. But every one of them seems to be having a lot of fun, too. And little things like the names on Main Street or the crests in the castle or the tombstones at the Haunted Mansion help that along.

"And that's the message I want to take back to my company. We're very serious about what we do, and that's as it should be. It's helped us gain a reputation for outstanding performance. But I think lately we've begun to take ourselves too seriously."

"Distribution is a tough business. People feel that because it's so tough we have to be serious. But you can be serious without being solemn. I want people to enjoy coming to work, to look forward to it. When we hit one of these tough spots, that's when we need a sense of humor to bounce back."

She could see that everyone agreed with her.

"Also, in both health care and distribution, consolidation is going on every day. Mergers, acquisitions, you name it. All this competition and change can be scary at times, but I don't want us to get paralyzed with fear. I want us to have fun along the way.

"Probably every one of us feels our business is unique. And each one is. Bill, your bank, or Alan, your software firm. But we all face the same problems. That's another message that I'm getting loud and clear."

"Darn right," said Judy.

"But you know," Carmen said, "of all the things I'm learning, I think the first thing I'm going to do when I get back is to build in some of the fun things we used to do when we were smaller. It will be tricky, of course. We need to enjoy our work, but we also must make sure we don't stop being serious about results—quality and customer service. I figure the best way to do it is just tell them what I learned here and what I plan to do about it."

"I think that's an idea worth talking about," said Mort. "All of you have people in your companies who right now are wondering what you're learning here and how you're going to put it to work. At the very least, that makes them nervous—maybe even fearful. The easiest way to handle that is to deal with it up front. Tell them what you've picked up here. Let them know what your ideas are. And get feedback from them on how to make

the ideas work. This will help break the ice and over-
come the inertia."

Carmen glanced at her notes before she went on. "When
it got close to lunch time, I decided I was in the mood for
some authentic French cuisine, so I caught the monorail
over to Epcot and went to the French Pavilion.

"After ordering lunch, I started talking with a young
couple at the next table. I learned two things from them.
First, they were having a wonderful time. It was just
like going around the world, they said. I told them it
sounded like fun, but I have to confess, I was secretly
thinking, *Yeah, right.*

"Then the wife told me, 'We can't afford to go to
France or Italy, at least right now. But we *can* afford to come
here.' And then I realized the kind of magic this place
represents. These two hadn't deceived themselves into
thinking that this is the same as the real thing. Their
budget is limited, and later they probably *will* make it to
Europe, but for now the illusion is enough. After all, it is
a pretty good illusion, isn't it?

"They weren't at all naive, either. They had done
their homework. The husband asked me how I liked my
meal, and I told him it was very good. He agreed, commented on the freshness of the wild mushrooms, and
went on to say that each country's pavilion prepares
and serves its own authentic cuisine. There in the French
Pavilion, we were dining in a restaurant called Les Chefs

de France. It's run by three renowned French chefs," Carmen read from her notebook, " 'Paul Bocuse, Roger Vergé, and Gaston LeNôtre.' Now if that's not everyone and everything walking the talk, I don't know what is.

"That lunch conversation opened my eyes a little wider, and afterward I walked around some more and began to see things in a new light. The French Pavilion is modeled on La Belle Epoque, and I began to believe that life in that era must have felt very much like this, at least to some of the more prosperous French.

"It reminded me of something my college history professor said: 'Tell me, and I forget. Show me, and I remember. Involve me, and I understand.' That's what I felt about the French Pavilion: it involved me. I stopped thinking of it as just a place to have lunch and began to enjoy the moment—something I need to do more of.

"Oh, one other thing I learned from that young couple was about Port Orleans, where they were staying. The theme there is the French Quarter in New Orleans. They said it has good restaurants and a lovely swimming pool built around a sea serpent. But I especially liked what they told me about the rooms.

"Each room has framed photographs and portraits on the walls that give it a homey feel. This couple mentioned to their housekeeper how much they liked the pictures. The housekeeper said, 'Oh, yeah, those are my parents, and this is my husband, and that's my daughter.' That's how they learned that cast members use their own family pictures in the rooms.

"That made me feel so good. I thought to myself, *What a warm touch.* And what a sense of ownership. It wasn't a hotel room anymore—it was a room that had real family photos in it. The hotel rooms involve the cast members in a very direct way.

"I realize now that as our company has grown, we've lost some of that sense of involvement. I'm going to get that back. I'm not sure how, because I'm not sure how it got away. But I do know I'm going to get it back. So that's the second thing I'm going to do.

"I'm also becoming more aware of how details affect our relationships with our customers. Most details are small, many go almost unnoticed, yet together they have such a big effect. We've been charging ahead, being very competitive, acquiring customers. But after we get them, we sometimes let the details slip, and soon they're someone else's customers. We have to do a better job of looking after those customers once we acquire them.

"I have to confess that Sales—at least in our company—has a mindset that focuses more on acquiring customers and less on keeping them. We need to pay attention to the details that keep the customers we already have. As we learned from Bill, something like two-thirds of all Disney World guests are repeat guests. In part, it's the details that bring them back. I think that spending more time keeping customers would probably help profits.

"Now that doesn't mean we're going to ignore customer acquisition, because that's darned important. It's just that I'm going to get my team focusing more on keeping what we've got, getting more volume from each account—thinking share of customer instead of just share of market.

"Another thing that occurred to me is to look harder at the customers we *do* acquire. Like most companies, we spend too much time counting new customers. We need to change that. Here's a note I wrote to myself: 'It's more important to acquire the customers who count than it is to count the customers you acquire.' And that's just what we're going to do. We're going to look more carefully at getting the right customers.

"I'm also going to use your ideas about hiring and training, Judy. But I'm not going to stop there. I like the idea of building customer focus into everything—everyone walking the talk—so I'm going to promote Alan's idea of giving everyone a 'Customer Relations' business card at my company. If I'm any good at sales, I should be able to demonstrate the value of that to my boss.

"I'm sure I'll come up with more ideas by the time I get back to work. Guess that's about it for now. Oh—except for one other thing. Mort, can I say something now about those twelve things my kids found at Wilderness Lodge?"

"Well, I guess—" Mort began, but he was interrupted by a short, sharp whistle. Everybody turned and looked at Don, who had his finger to his lips. He winked.

Mort seemed pleased. "I'm sorry, Carmen," he said. "Don says we have to wait."

BUILDING STRONG BUSINESS PARTNERSHIPS

Day 3, 2:45–3:00 P.M.

Mort slowly turned to Alan. "Okay," he said. "Now the one without the top hat."

Alan smiled and moved to the front of the group. "Well, I was hoping to have a guest speaker for you, but he hasn't shown up yet, so first I'll tell you a story of my own and then an observation I've made.

"A couple of years ago, my nephew took a basic computer class at our local community college. The instructor divided the class of twenty into four teams of five.

"Each team had to collect data from local sources, create a database, and generate spreadsheets, graphs, and other measures. Their final project was to present the work in notebook form. This represented 40 percent of each team member's final grade.

159

"My nephew, normally a rather casual student, was transformed. I can't remember his ever devoting as much time, energy, or commitment as he did to that class. Afterward, I noticed that he seemed easier to communicate with, and that he was a better team player in basketball.

"He learned those skills—people skills—in real time, while involved with a seemingly unrelated project. I was curious about his instructor. I asked around, and I discovered that he had been teaching this class for many years. Area companies scrambled to hire his students, as much for their team skills as anything else.

"I was reminded of this by the round tables used in Traditions to promote teamwork. In my nephew's class, a large part of each student's grade depended on how well he or she worked with other students. So that's my first lesson.

"One thing I'm going to do back at the office is promote some of this real-time learning about teamwork. In our sales training classes, we'll seat people in the round. When we get Inside Sales together with Field Sales, we'll have them work in teams on real tasks. I like the round tables so much that I'm going to get one for the new conference room where we meet suppliers and customers.

"The other thing is just a quick observation about what we've picked up here. We're from companies that range from small to large. But what we're picking up here applies to any business. My wife is a good example. She's in the process of leaving her job and starting her own business. Now, one thing we learned on our first day here is that, in the eyes of a customer, a home-based business is judged the same as Disney, FedEx, and L. L. Bean too. That first lesson applies just as much to her as it does to any of us! In fact, even as I'm saying this, I realize that it applies to my nephew. He's in real estate, and his clients make the same phone calls we talked about earlier. He's not going to be happy when I tell him who he competes with, but he should understand that his competition is heavier than he thinks it is.

"And now I see that my guest speaker has arrived. Excuse me for a moment."

Alan got up and walked over to a man who had strolled into the area and seemed to be looking for someone. The muscular, dark-haired man was wearing dark slacks and a polo shirt.

"I thought he was kidding," said Judy.

"This is Randy Dent," said Alan. They all stood and introduced themselves to Randy and said they were glad he could join them. Alan made room for Randy beside him on the bench.

"First, a little background," said Alan to the group. "I was strolling down Main Street, not noticing the names that Bill saw on the second-story businesses. I didn't see the T-shaped planter-sprinklers either. But I did notice something that I had walked by many times before without seeing—the Story of Walt Disney.

"This attraction is all about Walt's life and accomplishments—his movies, his Oscars, photos taken with Laurel and Hardy and other friends. It's something I want my kids to see—how one man's dream resulted in all this.

"After I left there, I sat on a bench to think about your assignment, Mort, but I soon found myself talking with this guy sitting next to me. Before long he said to me, 'You're not a regular guest here, are you?' I said no and explained what we were doing.

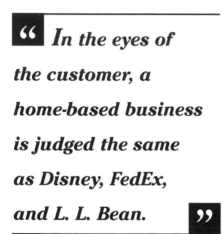

❝ *In the eyes of the customer, a home-based business is judged the same as Disney, FedEx, and L. L. Bean.* ❞

"Then he proceeded to tell me a story. It was a pretty darned good story and it covered a lot of what we've been discussing. So I invited him here to tell you what he told me.

"First, you should know that Randy is no ordinary guest, either. He's a former cast member who's back for a visit. He was part of the Disney communications team during the construction of Epcot.

"Randy, would you please tell my friends what you told me?"

Randy began. "Well, I'm very flattered that Alan thought my story was interesting enough to share with a class of school kids." They laughed. "And I'll try to remember exactly what I told him.

"Anyway, the whole thing happened because Disney is one of the few organizations in the world that will pick a specific date years in advance and say we are going to open on that date. 'On October 1, 1971, we are going to open Walt Disney World.' 'On October 1, 1982, we are going to open Epcot.' They advertise it and they make no bones about it.

"Epcot was the largest private construction project in the world at that time. It has since been dwarfed by a lot of other projects, but it was a very large project then. Most of the people working on it did not work for Disney; they worked for all these contractors and subcontractors. Construction workers typically have no special allegiance to any particular project. One month they'll be working on a high-rise in New York, the next month on a dam in Utah, and after that they're at Epcot.

"What Disney decided to do, and this is a unique Disney way of doing things, was to make these workers feel as though they were part of the Disney family—to get them to identify with Epcot even though they weren't actually part of the Disney organization. This had never been done before.

"Here's how they did it. They closed down the job site one Sunday a month for over a year. Now, keep in mind that this was the world's biggest construction project, they were moving toward a rock-solid deadline, so to shut the place down one day a month was a big deal.

"Disney brought in several big circus tents and set them up in what was eventually to be the Epcot parking lot. Food service went in one of the tents. We cooked hot dogs and hamburgers and served Cokes, potato chips, the whole works. In other words, we had a picnic.

"In another tent, we created a miniature Epcot. We brought in designers, the art department, the pavilion sponsors. We sculpted the ground to show where the land and the water would be. We put up photographs of the work as it progressed. We had artists' renderings to show everybody what it would look like when it was finished, and we stationed someone there to explain each pavilion. We kept everything up to date. We compacted the road going around the center of Epcot, so that the trams could drive on it.

"On that one Sunday a month, we'd shut down, and all the construction workers would bring their families, and we'd throw them a picnic and let them look around. They'd enjoy the food and then they'd walk through the tents and the whole family could see what Dad, or in some cases Mom, was doing.

"I would stand there and watch all of this. I won't kid you—some of those people scared the heck out of me. Those laborers were some of the roughest-looking guys I ever hope to meet. But these Hell's Angels, bikers, tough guys, they'd bring their girlfriends and their wives and their kids, and the kids would run around screaming, 'This is where Daddy works, this is Daddy's building.' After they went through the pavilions, they'd get on the trams and ride around the site. And I knew we were creating pride and ownership in the project.

"We did this every month so the families could watch it grow and the workers could see what they were creating—not just the big picture, but where their piece happened to fit into the big picture.

"Another thing we did, we created a weekly newspaper called the *Epcot Center Construction News.* Everywhere I went I carried two cameras and a bag of film. I'd walk up to a group of men working on something and shoot a group picture and write down their names and home towns. We published this newspaper every week like clockwork for a year and a half. It was loaded with photos. I'd have twenty or thirty pictures in every issue, probably four or five hundred people a month.

"I would also go to a different pavilion each time and interview the foreman to get the status of the work. We didn't just do the show areas, either. We went behind the scenes and did stories on the electrical contractor, the underground wiring, the wastewater system, things like that. One story was on the monorail. I went off property to the factory where they cast the beams, then showed how the beams were put on trucks and hauled to the site.

"This went on all the way through the construction cycle until Epcot opened. The project came in on time and on budget, with very few snags. This was in part thanks to thousands of people who were not cast members.

"We weren't writing their paychecks. We weren't giving them benefits. We couldn't do the traditional things that you do to keep employees happy.

"So, what could we do? We *treated* them like cast members. That's what we did. And it worked. I still remember the day Epcot opened, the grand opening celebration. It was a huge event. And just about all the people who worked on the project were there with their families."

"Tell them about the Land Pavilion," said Alan.

"Sure. One day, Dick Nunis and I were driving around in a golf cart checking on construction. This was about six months before opening day. We drove to the Land Pavilion, which has a large atrium with a restaurant in the bottom. In the atrium there are several huge mobiles that rise and fall slowly on cables hanging from the ceiling. They represent things about the land—harvest time, growing time, and so forth.

"The designer was not pleased. The pieces of the mobile were supposed to stay facing in one direction, but as winches raised and lowered them, the cables would twist and the pieces would spin slowly around. Several engineers were standing around scratching their heads. Nobody could figure out a way to keep the cables from twisting.

"There was a laborer nearby, sweeping up sawdust. He leaned on his broom and said, 'I used to work on an oil derrick. The cables we used didn't twist. Had to do with the weave.'

"Nunis and all these engineers stood there for a minute and didn't say a word. Then Nunis turned to the head engineer and said, 'Check it out.' The guy scribbled a bunch of notes and walked away. Nunis turned to the guy with the broom, asked his name, thanked him for the suggestion, and promised to try it.

"That's how they solved the problem. This was just a guy sweeping the floor, but the Disney organization will listen to anyone with a creative idea. Nunis is always looking for new ways to do things, creative solutions to problems, and that's why he's been so good for Disney. A lot of managers let their egos get in the way. If it's not their idea, it's no good. Nunis doesn't care where an idea comes from—cast member, guest, vice president, broom pusher. If it's good, he'll use it, and he'll give credit.

"So, Alan, is that what you wanted me to tell 'em?"

"That's it exactly, Randy. Thank you very much." Alan turned to the others. "I figured if Nunis could use other people's ideas, and if the American League can use a designated hitter, I could too. So I just let Randy be my designated hitter. That's fair enough, isn't it, Mort?"

"If you can bring back a story like that, why not?" Mort replied.

"Anyway," said Alan, "I spent the rest of my time walking around and thinking. I thought about my company and how we conduct business, the ways we market and distribute our products.

"We're a software company—a darn good one. But we tend to think of quality as being about *things.* We've got strategic alliances and partners. And we've done a good job of structuring the 'thing' part of those relationships. We have agreements; our computers talk to each other; we have partners' meetings. We do most of what the quality experts say you're supposed to do.

> **❝** *Quality is not about limited possibilities. Quality is about unlimited possibilities.* **❞**

"But until now, it would never have occurred to us to address a goal the way Disney did at Epcot. If we applied that same type of thinking to our external relationships, they'd be a lot stronger than they already are—and they're already pretty good.

"Here's what it boils down to. Quality is not about limited possibilities. Quality is about unlimited possibilities. If you start thinking about quality in terms of unlimited possibilities, it changes the way you think. So one of the things I'm going to do with my company is insist that everyone start thinking in terms of unlimited possibilities. And to make sure they understand what that means, I'm going to tell them what Randy just told us.

"Who knows where that will lead? I just know that we can take quality a lot further than we've taken it."

ONE WITH
PASSION . . .

Day 3, 3:00–3:15 P.M.

"**O**kay, Don, looks like your number's come up," said Mort.

Don hesitated. "Well, first, I have a confession to make. I don't know if you noticed, but I wasn't too pleased about being here. I value my time, and I don't like to waste it. I had to leave a lot of work stacked up to make this trip. But the boss insisted.

"Now, I can't say I haven't enjoyed and learned from parts of this outing, but this morning I still felt I was wasting good time. So I decided to check out one thing and then just make up some other stuff to fit.

"The one thing I wanted to check out was, what was it that Carmen was trying to tell us about Wilderness Lodge that Mort didn't want her to say? And why didn't Mort want her to tell us? Why is that, Mort?"

Mort smiled. "Because I was hoping someone would be curious enough to do a little independent research," he admitted.

"Well, it worked. I decided that whatever those twelve things were that didn't fit, I'd find them.

"So I went over to the lodge and started asking questions. I asked a couple of cast members if they knew of anything that wasn't in keeping with the Wilderness Lodge theme. They scratched their heads and said they couldn't think of anything—that everything was themed to our national parks in the West.

"Then a couple more cast members joined us there in the lobby, and before long we had a lively discussion going. I kept insisting that something here didn't match the theme and I wanted to know what it was. They kept insisting everything fit the theme.

"Finally I said to them, 'Hey, never mind. You guys don't have time to stand around and answer a bunch of Mickey Mouse questions.'

"As soon as I said that, one girl yelled, 'Mickey Mouse!' Then three others said, 'Yeah! That's it!'

"I said, '*What's* it?'

" 'Mickey Mouse!' said one of them. 'There are a dozen or more images of Mickey Mouse hidden in the details! They're called "hidden Mickeys." Here, I'll show you,' and she pointed to the enormous rock fireplace. I still didn't get it. She said, 'Look at the shape of the rocks on the right in that reddish layer about twenty feet off the ground.' Sure enough, if you looked closely you could make out the shape of Mickey's head and ears.

"Then they all started chiming in. 'When you go in the Cub's Den, look to the left of the teepee on the far wall.' I started writing down the places where they said there were hidden Mickeys, and, sure enough, among them they came up with twelve in and around the lodge. Turns out that every attraction, resort, and store has at least one hidden Mickey.

"According to the cast members, the hidden Mickeys started out as an inside joke by the Imagineers. In their designs and construction work, they would 'hide' Mickeys where they could be seen just as plain as the nose on your face, if you knew where to look.

"But no one kept track of them all. And as attractions are changed over the years, some are lost and others are added. But these cast members make a game of it. They compete to see who can find the most hidden Mickeys. They remind me of bird watchers who travel all over the world keeping lists and getting together to brag and compare notes."

"You're saying there are others besides the ones at Wilderness Lodge?" asked Alan.

"Do you play golf?" Don asked.

"Some would say not," Alan joked. "Want to join me after we finish up here?"

"Sure," said Don. "And if we play Magnolia, let's remember to check out the bunker on the sixth hole for a hidden Mickey. Or the putting green, if we go to Osprey

Ridge. And if any of you go back to It's a Small World—which I have no intention of doing unless threatened with bodily harm—look for the shadows cast by the ears of the baby kangaroo. They make a Mickey. Check out the blinders on the horses on Main Street. Splash Mountain has a Mickey Mouse cloud in the finale. Let's see. . . ." He squinted at his notebook. "I can't read my scribbling. . . .

"Oh, yes, I like this one. At Epcot, in the Norway Pavilion, there's a mural showing Norwegian history. One of the men in the mural is the Imagineer who designed the pavilion. And not only did the guy design himself into the mural, but he's wearing a Mickey Mouse watch. One of the Vikings is wearing Mickey Mouse ears.

"Any of you take your kids to see *The Lion King*?" he asked. Judy and Carmen nodded yes. "When you rent the video, watch closely when the ants march across the screen. One of them is wearing ears."

"Hey, Don?" said Carmen. "Can I get a list of the Mickeys you found? I want to impress my kids."

"You'll never be able to read my writing. In fact, I can't make out some of these notes myself. I'll type up a list and fax it to you later, okay?

"Anyway, I left the Wilderness Lodge with several pages of notes about hidden Mickeys but not much else. All this was amusing, but I was at a loss to find anything significant in it. I know you've talked about attention to detail, Mort, but I'm accustomed to thinking in terms of priorities. Sometimes things happen so fast in our business that we have to perform a sort of triage, take care of the emergencies first and let the details wait.

"So I came back over here and wandered around some more, went through a couple of attractions, bought a hot dog and sat on a bench watching all these outrageously happy people go by.

"Then, while I was sitting there, I saw this little carrot-top kid who seemed to be having a good time. And I remembered, I had seen her before, our first day here—couldn't miss her with those Mickey Mouse sunglasses and the big Goofy hat with the floppy ears. When we sat in the restaurant having coffee, I saw her through the window. She was pretty unhappy then—remember?

"So I approached these people, showed them my badge and letter, and told them what I was doing here. I said I had seen their little girl—her name's Nancy—crying about something a couple of days before and that I was glad to see she was having a good time now."

Don paused to scan the group's reaction. "Here's what they told me. Nancy had been standing in line waiting to get Captain Hook's autograph. Just as her turn came, Captain Hook suddenly disappeared. This made her instantly unhappy, and she burst into tears and could not be consoled. So they left the attraction.

"The father stopped a cast member to complain about Hook's rude behavior. The cast member apologized and said that when one Captain Hook's shift ends, he's supposed to be relieved by another Captain Hook. Apparently there was a mix-up, and the fresh Hook didn't take his place quickly enough. The cast member asked where the family was staying and said he would try to make things right for Nancy.

"When Nancy got back to her room, there was a Peter Pan doll and a note on her bed. The note said, 'Dear Nancy, I'm very sorry that Captain Hook was mean to you today. Some days he is mean to me, too. Please come back and visit us real soon. Your friend, Peter Pan.'

"She was so excited. Peter Pan had flown up to their room and left a note on her bed!

"I was very impressed at the efficiency of this operation. In the short time it took them to get back to the Contemporary Hotel for lunch and for Nancy's nap, a lot of things happened. The cast member they complained to phoned the hotel and got someone there to write a note. That someone also rounded up a doll and then arranged for housekeeping to leave the doll and the note in the room.

"Now, earlier I saw something else. I was somewhere in or near Fantasyland. There was a woman holding an ice cream cone. She was busy talking with her friend. A gull swooped down and knocked the ice cream to the ground, and about a dozen more gulls came out of nowhere and landed on it.

"A cast member saw all this. Immediately she escorted the woman to the front of the ice cream line and got her a new ice cream cone.

"I stopped the woman with the ice cream and asked her about it. At first she thought I was a reporter. Even after I explained what I was doing and that the only reporting I would do would be to a few others like myself, she insisted on giving me her name and her phone number, in case I wanted her picture for my story.

"Now those were both situations where a problem got corrected—one where a cast member made a mistake and one where a gull caused the problem. And they both got corrected fast and effectively. How do they do that, Mort?"

"It's a process called Service Recovery," said Mort. "When something doesn't go the way someone expects, the cast goes to extra lengths to make it right. They don't want anyone to go away disenchanted, so they make it a practice to bring things back to a state of balance. I believe that it's crucial in maintaining guest loyalty. It also helps keep cast members committed because it gives them the opportunity to fix things right on the spot for that guest. As with everything else, Disney puts a lot of time and energy into a good recovery, but it's well worth the effort.

"But I'd like to hear more about your walkabout. What do you conclude from what you saw? And how will it affect what you do back on the job?"

Don was silent for a moment, gathering his thoughts. When he looked up, it was as if all the tension he'd been carrying for the past few days had drained out of him. He even began his speech with a smile.

The others smiled back spontaneously, and waited.

"Well, as I said, I was having trouble seeing the relevance of any of this to my work and my business. I mean, some of it was interesting, sure, but to me— bottom line—it was basically just a scavenger hunt for oddball facts and strange practices. Then something happened.

"I was sitting on a bench and was about ready to start over here when this couple sits down next to me so the woman can tie her shoelace. The guy says something to her about how clean this place is. She agrees, and they start guessing how many custodians there must be. She says 300. He says it must be more like 400 or 500. At this point, I can't resist.

"So I tell them 45,000. Naturally, they're amazed. I let them be amazed for a little bit. Then I explain why, and how, I know.

"Now they're even more amazed. 'You know,' the guy says to me, 'if more people in more companies had that same dedication to *their* customers, their companies would be more profitable, their jobs would be more secure, and I'd be a happier customer. Not that many people have that same degree of passion about making things right for their customers.' And with that, they get up, say good-bye, and leave.

"What happened was the guy said 'passion.' And when he said that, it triggered something inside me. It reminded me of something my high school football coach once said.

"I wasn't the most talented or most coordinated athlete on the team, but I always played my heart out. In my junior year, I had to share the right guard position with another player. He usually started, and I sat on the bench a lot. But I always went full out—even in practice—and although I seldom started, I almost always played.

"One day at practice, things weren't going so well. Everyone was pretty much just going through the motions. I was hitting hard, but thinking about slacking off. Then the coach whistled us off the field and called us over to the sideline.

"I can still see him standing on the bench, and I can still hear his voice. He said, 'How many of you are interested in winning Friday night's game?'

"Forty-one hands went up.

"'Well, I've got bad news for you,' he said. 'Being interested isn't enough. A lot of people are interested in a lot of things. I'm interested in winning the Boston Marathon. But you know what? I'm never going to win the Boston Marathon. I'm not committed to it. I'm not *passionate* enough about it. That's what it takes—passion and commitment! And you guys are about as far

> **❝ *If there were more people in more companies with real dedication to their customers, their companies would be more profitable and their jobs more secure.* ❞**

from being passionate and committed as anyone I know of. In fact, there's only one player that I can see who's showing any passion at all, and that's Jenkins.

" 'But I'll tell you one thing,' he continued. 'I'm passionate about Friday night's game. I'm so passionate about it that I'm going to make you a promise. Everybody on that field Friday night will have passion and commitment.

" 'Right now I have one starter. One. That's Jenkins. I will not put anyone on the field who does not have a passion for winning. If Jenkins is the only one on the field, then so be it. One with passion is better than forty who are merely interested.'

"And with that, he stalked off the field, and the assistant coach ran the rest of the practice.

"Well, I started that Friday, and it was one of our biggest games of the season. We won, thirty-five to six. I started every game after that. I lettered in both my junior and senior years.

"I realized immediately why I was suddenly thinking about the coach. I had seen that same passion in the cast members who were helping me find the hidden Mickeys. Even when they couldn't figure out what the heck I was talking about, they were enthusiastic and engaged. Everyone seemed passionate about helping find whatever it was, even though I didn't have a clue.

"I also realized that I had seen it in the cast member who talked about the letters on the bulletin board. And in Michael Eisner—and in each of you." He paused.

"So go on," said Mort. "Tell us how you're going to apply this back at work."

Don thought for a moment. "Well, I think we've done a great job about product quality at my company. We've got numbers we watch every day. We're passionate about those things. But that's not the same thing as

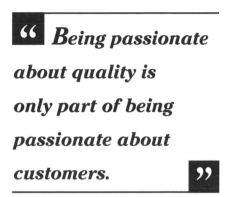

❝ *Being passionate about quality is only part of being passionate about customers.* **❞**

being passionate about *customers.* Being passionate about quality is only part of being passionate about customers.

"That's what's going on here. People are passionate about a guest's experience. The vehicles for making that a great experience are all the things we've been talking about. I couldn't see how gold-leaf paint or the mural or Traditions or any of that made a difference for my team. The truth of the matter is that they don't—for me.

"But they *do* make a difference here. Those things are all about fun and magic, and that's what this place is all about—fun and magic.

"They all contribute to the total experience, and that's what counts. I mean, let's face it, this is not the cheapest place in the world to visit. As for me person-ally, I could never get as excited about it as you do, Judy. But when you get right down to it, you've gotta admit that the people at Disney do deliver value.

"That's what all businesses have to do. Disney has to deliver value, and so do we. It's so deceptively simple that I missed it.

"Which is a roundabout way of saying that my action plan is really only one step long. I'm going to take the same passion I've had for quality and simply convert it into a passion for each customer's total experience. It's a small change in the words, but it's going to produce a big change in the way we do things and in the way our customers experience us. That change alone will pay for the whole trip.

"And thanks for putting up with me. I hope it was worth it."

Judy smiled and shook his hand. "I knew you'd come around."

As the rest of the Gang of Five chatted and prepared to go their separate ways, Carmen made one last entry in her notebook:

"One with passion is better than forty who are merely interested."

She smiled, thinking of Don.

LEADER'S

TOOL KIT

How to Put the Lessons to Work in Your Company

The people who read this book before it went to the type-setter and printer were from all different types and sizes of organizations. One was from a small community service organization, another from an advertising agency. Two were presidents of small to medium-sized companies, and four were training directors in large companies. But they—and the eight other "outside" readers—all had a common request: a vehicle for them to use with other people on their team to, as one of them put it, "leapfrog the competition."

That's what this tool kit is about. It's a way to help you make customer focus as much a part of the way you do business as it is part of the way Disney does business. The people we tested it on found that it helped build team spirit, sharpen customer focus, and improve their systems.

You can use this tool kit as part of a training program, as part of a "lunch and learn" program, or to examine how you do business with either internal or external customers.

In short, this tool kit is a way for you to create your own think tank. Gather a group of employees from across different organizational functions or from your functional area. Get your management team together. If you're a one-person business, hold the discussion with yourself—or with four to seven other people who are also in business for themselves. If you meet with a study group, use that vehicle to examine alternatives. Everyone experiences this material differently. By conducting a discussion, you'll encourage the comparison of differing perceptions, enhance creative problem solving, and increase receptivity to new ideas.

Preparing for the Discussion

Discussions work best in small groups of five or six individuals. If you're working with a large audience, ask people to meet in small groups, discuss and record their ideas, then reconvene to share conclusions. A circular seating arrangement promotes interaction.

Prepare a list of the discussion questions. Write two or three questions on a flip chart for display during the discussion. Use questions from the list or generate your own. Use large lettering. The purpose of displaying the questions is to keep the group on track, much the way you would use a meeting agenda.

Share the questions with the participants prior to the discussion. This will give them time for reflection and allow them to refer to particular sections of the book. You may wish to ask them to add other questions to the list.

Leading the Discussion

Post the questions in full view of all the participants.

Pose one question at a time. After the conversation gets moving, try to take a back seat. Give the group control of the discussion. Avoid repeating the question unless the group gets off track—then refer back to the posted question. If people seem to be holding back, bring them into the discussion with a question: "Peg, what do you think about this?" Record all ideas suggested.

Summarize. Before you proceed to the next question, briefly summarize the main points you have discussed. Refer to the points that you captured in writing.

QUESTIONS

LESSON 1:
The competition is anyone the customer compares you with.

◆ Recall a situation where you were very impressed with the level of service you received. How did it raise your expectations of other companies?

◆ How does our company's service compare?

◆ Who are our direct competitors?

◆ Who else might our customers compare us with?

◆ What does that suggest about how we might change the way we do business?

LESSON 2:
Pay fantastic attention to detail.

◆ What details get in the way of our being easy to do business with?

- ◆ What details could be improved to keep our customers coming back?
- ◆ What details in our workplace could become "hitching posts"?

LESSON 3:
Everyone walks the talk.

- ◆ Think about the *way* people do their jobs here. Could we adapt the "aggressively friendly" concept to our company's environment?
- ◆ How might we expand customer service from a department to a tradition?
- ◆ How could we individually do an even better job of "walking the talk" than we do right now?
- ◆ What does "walking the talk" mean around here?
- ◆ How would a customer's experience be different if everyone here "walked the talk"?

LESSON 4:
Everything walks the talk.

- ◆ Remember the gold-leaf paint on the carousel. What messages are being sent to our associates/employees about the value of customers?
- ◆ Keeping in mind the importance of things unseen, in what ways could we remind employees that customers are "pure gold"?
- ◆ Imagine that everything in our company walked the talk. What would that look like?
- ◆ What's one thing that could be changed so that it did a better job of walking the talk?

LESSON 5:
Customers are best heard through many ears.

- How can we "put on our ears" to track customer satisfaction?

- How could the process of gathering feedback be more creative and fun?

- Remember the impact of immediate action. How could we improve our response time?

- Identify and list aspects of our job(s) that involve customer contact. (Best used for a homogeneous discussion group.)

- What formal or informal listening posts are we not using that we could be using?

- How could we become more responsive to customer needs?

LESSON 6:
Reward, recognize, and celebrate.

- How often does good performance go unrecognized?

- In general, what's the positive-to-negative feedback ratio in our company/plant/department/etc.?

- How could we improve that ratio?

- What is your individual ratio of positive-to-negative feedback?

LESSON 7:
Xvxryonx makxs a diffxrxncx.

- Thinking about the typewriter with the broken key, how could our company apply this lesson?

- In what ways have we personally experienced this lesson?

- How can we communicate this belief to others in the company?

GENERAL QUESTIONS

◆ What is the main message of this book?

◆ What insights have you gained from reading this book?

◆ What's the one thing you're going to do differently, starting today?

Ending the Discussion

In one or two sentences, state what you have accomplished as it relates to the initial questions posed. If the ultimate goal of your discussion is application, create an action plan that includes who, what, and when.

NOTES

◆

If you did not read "About This Book," you have probably guessed anyway that Mort and his "Gang of Five" are creatures of my imagination. Any similarity between them and anyone you know is coincidental. Mort, for example, is a vehicle for describing what goes on at Disney and adding his (my) comments. I have never worked for Disney in any capacity.

With three exceptions—Michael Eisner, Dick Nunis, and Judson Green—all the Disney cast member names are also fictional. All the Disney "factoids" are true. The seven lessons are also real—but they are my reality. Each lesson is my observation about how Disney—and other intensely customer-focused companies—do things. For example, as far as I know, Disney does not hand out a card that says "Xvxryonx makxs a diffxrxncx." That's simply my way of describing the importance they ascribe to each individual cast member as well as the importance you should ascribe to every member of your team.

As you might guess, Disney is a fascinating organization to observe. If you'd like to find out more about the Disney approach to leadership, people management, or service quality, contact Disney Institute, 1960 Magnolia Way, Lake Buena Vista, FL 32830. Telephone: 407-827-1100.

FURTHER READING

◆

Enhancing your customer-focus skills is a never-ending process. With that in mind, we offer the following short listing of books, newsletters, games, training videos, and seminars.

BOOKS AND ARTICLES

Anderson, Kristin. *Great Customer Service on the Telephone.* New York: AMACOM Books, 1992.

Anderson, Kristin, and Ron Zemke. *Coaching Knock Your Socks Off Service.* New York: AMACOM Books, 1996.

Anderson, Kristin, and Ron Zemke. *Delivering Knock Your Socks Off Service.* New York: AMACOM Books, 1991.

Anderson, Kristin, and Ron Zemke. *Knock Your Socks Off Answers: Solving Customer Nightmares and Soothing Nightmare Customers.* New York: AMACOM Books, 1995.

Bell, Chip R. *Customers As Partners: Building Relationships That Last.* San Francisco: Berrett Koehler, 1994.

Bell, Chip R. *Managers As Mentors: Building Partnerships for Learning.* San Francisco: Berrett Koehler, 1996.

Bell, Chip R., and Ron Zemke. *Managing Knock Your Socks Off Service.* New York: AMACOM Books, 1992.

Berry, Leonard L. *On Great Service: A Framework for Action.* New York: Free Press, 1995.

Charles, C. Leslie. *The Customer Service Companion: The Essential Handbook for Those Who Serve Others.* East Lansing. Yes!Press, 1996.

Cook, Susan, and Roger Dow. *Turned On: Eight Vital Insights to Energize Your People, Customers, and Profits.* New York: Harper Business, 1996.

Connellan, Thomas K. *Sustaining Knock Your Socks Off Service.* New York: AMACOM Books, 1993.

Flower, Joe. *Prince of the Magic Kingdom: Michael Eisner and the Re-Making of Disney.* New York: John Wiley and Sons, Inc., 1991.

Freiberg, Kevin, and Jackie Freiberg. *NUTS! Southwest Airlines' Crazy Recipe for Business and Personal Success.* Austin: Bard Press, 1996.

Greene, Katherine, Richard Greene, and Katherine Barrett. *The Man behind the Magic: The Story of Walt Disney.* New York: Penguin Group, 1991.

Grover, Ron. *The Disney Touch: How a Daring Management Team Revived an Entertainment Empire.* New York: Richard D. Irwin, Inc., 1991.

Johnson, Rich. "A Strategy for Service—Disney Style." *Journal of Business Strategy,* September/October 1991.

The Project on Disney. *Inside the Mouse: Work and Play at Disney World.* Durham: Duke University Press, 1995.

Reichheld, Frederick R. *The Loyalty Effect: The Hidden Force behind Growth, Profits, and Lasting Value.* Boston: Harvard Business School Press, 1996.

Smith, Dave. *Disney A to Z: The Official Encyclopedia.* New York: Hyperion, 1996.

Stratton, Brad. "How Disneyland Works." *Quality Progress,* July 1991.

Zemke, Ron. *The Service Edge: 101 Companies That Profit from Customer Care.* New York: New American Library, 1989.

Zemke, Ron. *Service Recovery: Fixing Broken Customers.* Portland, Oreg.: Productivity Press, 1995.

OTHER RESOURCES

Creating and Managing Distinctive Quality Service. Video presentation with Chip R. Bell. Performance Research Associates, Minneapolis, Minn.

Customers from Hell and the Ten Deadly Sins of Customer Care Board Game. Performance Research Associates, Inc., Minneapolis, Minn.

Managing Extraordinary Service. Customized training program offered by Kaset Inc., Tampa, Fla.

Who's the Competition? Video presentation with Tom Connellan. Performance Research Associates, Minneapolis, Minn.

ACKNOWLEDGMENTS

◆

Every author says "I couldn't have done it without so and so." And it's always true. Especially with this book.

First, a big thank-you to the present and former cast members who gave of their time and allowed me to interview them. Their roles were diverse—including both Parks and Resorts, senior vice president, editor of *Eyes and Ears,* numerous characters, driver of the old-time cars, and guest relations. Of particular note are Corey Cohen, Mike Turner, Keith Gossett, Kerry Price, Terri Cooksey, and Ani Costa. Special thanks to Drew Turner, who although not a cast member, was invaluable in helping me complete my research.

Credit for work on the Leader's Tool Kit goes to Deb Woudenberg, Doug Kerfoot, Dan Houston, Bill Stimer, and Kristi Heyboer.

The Bard Press team was superb. Without them, you wouldn't have this book. Ray Bard, Scott Bard, Nancy Thomas, and Karen Kobe were outstanding. The editing, design, and production team of Jeff Morris, Leslie Stephen, Carolyn Banks, Suzanne Pustejovsky, Deborah Costenbader, Doreen Piano, and Sherry Sprague brought the ideas to life.

Robert Blaha, Clay Cary, Caryn Colgan, Sheryl Horton, Stacey Crowley, John Murphy, Cherise Person, Ed Pope, Sara Schroeder, Kay Scott, Alan Sultan, Buddy Tune, and Mike Turner all took valuable time from their own jam-packed schedules to read the manuscript and give valuable feedback. Also, thanks to the many people who provided feedback on various combinations of titles and subtitles.

My three partners, Kristin Anderson, Chip Bell, and Ron Zemke, also read the manuscript—not just one version, but three separate versions. Their very direct and insightful comments were needed and appreciated. I'm never sure how they find time to be so supportive with all they have on their own plates, but they always do, and I love them for it. Jill Applegate and Karen Revill somehow manage to keep the four of us headed in the right direction—even though it must be like herding cats. Thanks for your constant support. Additional thanks to our supplementary support staff, Peppy and Kippy, whose ongoing attention to every detail of this project was invaluable.

So who's left? Pam, for one—my loving wife, who not only endured the alarm going off at 5:30 every morning, but also three consecutive trips through It's a Small World to recheck one final fact. And my daughter, Avis, who not only gave me feedback on the cover design but also gives me feedback on even more important things. Plus Pam's two sons, Scott and Doug.

Thanks to everyone!

ABOUT THE AUTHOR

◆

If you're wondering what to do when your competition is only a click away, **Tom Connellan** probably has the answers—he's one of North America's leading authorities on creating and maintaining customer-centric organizations.

A senior partner with Performance Research Associates and a Guest Lecturer at The University of Michigan, Tom draws on the hundreds of focus groups and surveys he and his partners have run to help clients create a laser-like focus on customers. That's why customer-focused firms like Marriott, Raytheon, Neiman-Marcus, Merck, Lucent, Merrill Lynch, GE, IBM, Sony, and Dell regularly use Tom to help them forge even stronger links with their customers.

Tom's work includes the topic areas of:
- managing customer relationships,
- using technology to interface with customers,
- enhancing customer loyalty,
- retaining at-risk customers,
- sharpening customer focus,
- shaping the appropriate people-customer-profit links,
- building customer-centric organizations,
- and creating customer-focused agility.

Tom brings a unique and distinctive perspective to his work. He is a former faculty member at The University of Michigan where he served as a Research Associate and

Program Director in the Business School's Executive Education program. He also served as the Editorial Director of four management and human resource journals.

Tom is the author of six books and numerous articles. An active Silicon Valley investor, he is on the Advisory Board of several Internet start-ups.

No stranger to the firing line of business, Tom started a service company in the health care field. Using an intense focus on the customer, he built it into a network of 1200 instructors serving 300 hospitals and most of the Fortune 500 firms. In two different reports, the Surgeon General cited the firm's quality.

As an entrepreneur, investor, author, and researcher, Tom brings a solid background to his work with companies seeking to build stronger relationships with their customers.

For information on Tom's availability to keynote your conference, call 734-998-1414.

PERFORMANCE RESEARCH ASSOCIATES, INC.

◆

Performance Research Associates (PRA) is one of North America's premier consulting firms in the area of customer loyalty. From its offices in Minneapolis, Dallas, and Ann Arbor, it provides training and consulting services to clients in North and South America, Europe, and the Pacific Rim. The three senior partners of PRA—Chip Bell, Tom Connellan, and Ron Zemke—have collectively authored 33 books and more than 1,100 articles.

PRA partners regularly make presentations and conduct training sessions for organizations who want to enhance individual, team, and organizational performance. These presentations fall into the areas of leadership, customer loyalty, and change. Each presentation is tailored to the organization's needs.

PRA also regularly works with companies to assess not only customer loyalty but also the degree of customer focus in the organization. They also help companies resolve organizational issues that hinder team effectiveness and customer loyalty. Many of these projects involve developing systems that increase the retention of at-risk customers. Other projects involve helping client organizations reinvent their service system and develop service strategies.

For information about PRA services, call 734-998-1414.

VISIT YOUR FAVORITE BOOKSTORE
FOR ADDITIONAL COPIES OF

INSIDE THE MAGIC KINGDOM
Seven Keys to Disney's Success

$20 Hardcover

OR

Call Toll-free

1-800-945-3132

Or fax

(512) 288-5055

24 hours a day

Seven days a week

VISA/MasterCard/American Express/Discover accepted

Quantity discounts are available.

A BARD PRESS BOOK

Project coordinator   Nancy Thomas
Executive editor   Leslie Stephen
Developmental editor   Jeff Morris
Consulting editor   Carolyn Banks
Copy editor   Deborah Costenbader
Word processing   Sherry Sprague
Proofreaders   Deborah Costenbader
                         Doreen Piano

Text design   Suzanne Pustejovsky
Composition   Round Rock Graphics
Jacket design   Suzanne Pustejovsky